OF TRUTH AND TERRORISM

OF TRUTH AND TERRORISM

Gp Capt. (R) Rab Nawaz Choudhry

authorHOUSE®

AuthorHouse™
1663 Liberty Drive
Bloomington, IN 47403
www.authorhouse.com
Phone: 1-800-839-8640

First published by AuthorHouse   08/05/2011

ISBN: 978-1-4634-4916-2 (sc)
ISBN: 978-1-4634-4915-5 (hc)
ISBN: 978-1-4634-4914-8 (ebk)

Library of Congress Control Number: 2011914192

Printed in the United States of America

Table of Contents Page Numbers

Table of Contents   **Page Numbers**

Preface

Pakistan is passing through the most difficult times of its history.

There is no doubt that several nations have undergone similar and in some cases more severe circumstances. However, they came out of the whirlpool and have not only survived but have progressed to become strong member of committee of nations. The main reason for their survival and subsequent revival was the strong and selfless leadership who were sincere to their national cause. In the recent history China, Japan, Germany, Vietnam, Turkey, and Singapore are some of the glaring examples. A close study of these nations tell us that it was the ceaseless struggle of their leaders against all odds that built the confidence of the masses which supported their leaders and fought shoulder to shoulder with them. It has been a misfortune of Pakistan that few years after birth it has been confronted with a perpetual leadership crisis. Unfortunately our leaders became millionaires overnight through illegal means and corruption. Their loyalties to Pakistan can be judged from the mere fact that they have stacked their wealth in foreign banks.

The present day government is led by a person who was a symbol of corruption during his wife's rule. He has lowered the status of this country to such low levels that it has been termed as a "Failed State". His juggle-naught behavior compounded by the clownish performance of his ignorant Prime Minister and a group of courtier cabinet ministers has made Pakistan a laughing stock. The national fabric has been torn to pieces. Common Pakistani is disillusioned. He is not only demoralized but confronted with a sense of uncertainty in security and the future of his next generation.

The problem has been compounded by the intervention of some foreign powers who, taking advantage of our dilapidated position have decided to exploit the situation to their own advantage. Throwing peanuts in the begging bowls of these leaders, they have successfully made them to dance to their tunes. Like fools our leaders have taken the bait and conceded to the ever increasing demands of their masters "to do more" thus plunging the country into a quagmire in the name of terrorism. Terrorism and insurgency are two terms that have been grossly misused. While use of force and violence in any form is condemnable but labeling freedom movements and those fighting for their rightful rights as terrorists or insurgents is not justifiable. It is strange that when people rebel against their governments are termed as freedom fighters, while the same people when demand ouster of foreign forces from their land are labeled as terrorists.

I am of the strong belief that terrorism in the world cannot be eradicated until and unless the Palestinian issue is resolved. Majority of the Western Powers supported the existence of Israel because of the atrocities of Germans on Jews who needed to be provided a safe heaven. However, the principle of denying the Palestinians, their homeland to accommodate the internationally displaced Jews is not justifiable. Since all the western powers are great proponents of democracy, the solution of Palestine lies in following the democratic norms. Adopting the South African model in Palestine will help in resolving the problem.

During my service in the PAF and later after retirement I have had several opportunities of visiting USA and interacting of various factions of population there. I have found the common Americans peace loving people having full respect for the dignity of others irrespective of color, cast, and creed. I therefore decided to write an open letter to the common American to appeal to their conscience to impress upon their government to desist from meddling in the affair of other nations and upsetting the peace in these regions. The interference by the American government in internal matters of other countries is certain to have its repercussions, which directly or indirectly are likely to affect American people. The adventurous policies of the American government have already shown their affects in the form of economic pressures being faced where billions of dollars are wasted in bullying other nations, which could have been well spent on the welfare activities of its people like free medical treatment and old age pensions so badly needed by them. This open letter forms the first Chapter of my book.

I have tried to present naked truth in my book and a form of questionnaire to the American leadership leading to repair and return to normalcy. It will certainly pave the way to better understanding and relationship to establish peace everywhere.

Like any other Pakistani, who is pained to see his country's deteriorating condition; I have also suffered this anguish. I therefore felt duty bound to appeal to my countrymen through articles that I wrote from time to time where few of these were published by some newspapers but others, perhaps for reasons of backlash by concerned quarters, remain in the databanks of the editors. My present book is a compilation of these articles. My aim is to trigger the thought provoking process amongst my countrymen and other related countries like America, Iraq, and Afghanistan. How far I have succeeded in these efforts is for the readers to judge.

Gp. Capt. (R) Rab Nawaz Choudhry

Foreword

For the last over two decades the world has witnessed with concern, a strange phenomenon that has gradually engulfed largely the Muslim world into a perpetual state of crises. It is not a coincidence that the troubles that started from Lebanon in the eighties spread through Syria, Iran, Iraq, and Afghanistan & has now come into Pakistan. The recent upheavals in the Arab world also appear to be the part of this greater plan. Strange that it may seem the whole destabilisation effect is occurring in the area adjacent to Israel. Recent visit by the Israeli prime minister to USA & the stubbornness displayed by him provides food for thought.

Similarly a conflict exists in the western corridors regarding interpretation of terrorism. While in one place it is termed as freedom movement, similar use of force and under similar conditions is labelled as terrorism and dangerous for humanity and is used as an excuse to achieve political ends. History teaches us that stronger cannot keep the weaker suppressed forever. Reversal is inevitable. I hope the western leaders reread the dust laden history books stacked in their book shelves and take the lesson.

Group Captain Rab Nawaz as I have known him is an ardent patriotic Pakistani. A liberal person but he has the fundamentals of Islam very close to his heart. As a very sensitive person he could not stay aloof and unaffected by the events that were taking place around us, especially in Pakistan. He took up the pen to express the pain that he felt for his dear homeland in particular and the Islamic world in general. His courageous open letters to the rulers are in line with the famous saying that greatest Jihad is to speak the truth in the face of a tyrant. Many may not agree with his viewpoints but his sincerity of purpose and patriotism to Pakistan cannot be challenged. I hope the readers would view his book from this perspective.

Of Truth and Terrorism is a book of narrative of national and international events of current affairs. It concerns the recent history, and the outcome 9/11 resulting into the wars in Afghanistan, Pakistan, and Iraq. Al-Qaeda figured a central point that brought the whole conflict and triggered almost half of the world to form a coalition to chase the shadows of Al-Qaeda in Afghanistan and hostile hills of the tribal areas of Pakistan. The war, which was intended to last for a few months, has taken 10 long years and seems as fresh today as was kicked off in 2001. Chasing shadows is difficult and therefore the real victory is nowhere in sight. The orphans as the defeat defines them seem to be packing up their baggage back to the Base as was done in Vietnam. However, things could be changed with change of hearts and understanding. Choice I think is not with the muscles and might. The sooner they come to terms with logic and sanity the better it is for them and the world.

Mushtaq Ahmed Laghari
Air Vice Marshal (Retd.)
Former Ambassador of Pakistan
To
UNITED ARAB EMIRATES

An Open Letter to Common Americans

28ᵗʰ June 2006

You visit America once; meet ordinary people in the street or shopping malls, and you cannot help but say "Americans are great people." They are open, friendly, sympathetic, and honest in their dealings. Even sales people display inevitable attachment and sympathy towards customers and provide unerring shopping tips even if it negatively affects their own business. Their international dealings are exemplary and better than any other nation. This assessment is not simply out of cough; it is my personal observation after interaction with different people from almost 2/3 countries of the world. My faith in them stems down to even swearing about their character in day to day dealings. I am a staunch Muslim, non practicing, but whatever little knowledge I possess about Islam, I thought it was being practiced in America, except for the homosexuality, pornography, and vulgar night clubs.

I have some good friends and have kept in touch with them for the last twenty to thirty years. They are executives, businessmen, and common people like you, to whom I am addressing this letter today.

America is a big democracy. You also preach and patronize this concept throughout the world. You claim to be the leader of democracy in the world, and feel that freedom is synonymous with democracy. Your great forefathers discovered America in 1492 and called it a land of hope, fortune, aspiration, and above all, inspiration. The message sent back by these brave adventurists was not accepted in the same spirit it was meant to be. The people back home in Europe learned about the difficulties, hardships, struggles, and sufferings. Instead of reciprocating in good spirit, they put all of the criminals and mafias in the ships to get rid of them and forced them over to the newly founded country, America. However, these very criminals fought their way in unfriendly and hostile environments and organized themselves as a coherent force to establish in the new country; a future heaven and hope for all of you who form the U.S.A, as one of the proudest nations of the world today. In fact, the only super power of today. Unfortunately, as is the tradition of any new settlement, those very criminals became the leaders of the immigrants. They became rich, affluent, and strong. They declared themselves as all time in-charge of them at that time, and tried to change themselves through self reforms yet some sign of their original character always played and reflected whenever they got themselves involved in personal conflicts and feuds.

As time passed, people came to know the prospects and treasure of the new world. There was influx of all kinds of people who let their families gather fortune and return back home to enjoy. Most of them came, settled themselves, and never returned.

Those were your great grandfathers who fought for you. Many were killed over flimsy things, looted each other and committed many excesses on one another to believe that, Might was right. It appears that that very hereditary essence is working today in your leadership who unknowingly or unintentionally are acting on the same principle and destroying the peaceful mother earth. However, some or very few of the common people may be having the streak of that attribute, but I know the majority of you have noble blood in your veins. That is why the average and common American is so good in behavior, character, grain, quality, and above all their natural instinct.

The majority with all this noble nature must choose leaders with similar qualities and not from the earlier pedigree who have probably not transformed themselves like the common Americans. How about analyzing them before they destroy you or make this mother earth unworthy of living peacefully and with honor? You all need to look into that because it is you who matter today. Tomorrow, nobody has seen, but one can guess and speculate how it would look. However, don't forget as we sow, so shall we reap. The history has seen many such situations, super powers, dynasties, and empires. Where are they? They have gone, too soon and much before time. You are a great country and nation; we want you to stay much longer than all of the past abolished ones.

Leaving aside the internal strife that is part of such a large scale exodus, the only slur that I can point out in that ERA was the annihilation of the actual owners, the Native Americans. They should have been taken in to confidence and respected, but it was not done. However, the later invitations to all poor countries and their people to migrate, I feel, compensates the earlier follies committed. The second slur was the slave trade from Africa and inhumane behavior to those African Americans who also thought they were going towards the land of hope and fortune. Even this has been undone through force of their own conviction, but the credit goes to the common whites who supported African Americans to get their freedom and equal rights. Mind you, most of your leaders are still prejudice. Exceptions like Condoleezza Rice may not be enough proof to prove otherwise.

The history of Vietnam, Korea, and Japan presents ample proof of the originality of that nature and temper. The present events pursued by them also show the similar traditional effects of their character. If the common man does not get up and fight for change, I am afraid this system will continue till nature puts an end to it.

It is said that the taste of pudding lies in eating. Similarly, the leaders are also judged in times of crises. Their firmness, maturity, and strength of character can only be seen when the nation faces some kind of emergency crises. The tragedy since the initial Civil War, and a small battle with Canada and Mexico, where leaders like President James Madison and President George Washington were leading the country, America has had no serious crises facing the nation. 9/11 was the first test of the modern times, which really shook America to the core. How your present leadership coped with this crisis is a matter of your personal analysis and their accountability to the nation. I feel it is not for any intellectuals to prove or disprove their theories with all sorts of complicated and stupid thesis. A person in the street can see for themselves and draw a conclusion. In fact, a common and average person can do a better job of such things rather than the bookworms sitting around their laboratories and playing chess games with the sentiments and emotions of men and women in the street. The nation stands on small pillars of these poor people, but unfortunately, the decisions for these poor people's lives is taken by the small elite controlling and commanding the country. You, as a common person, at least have the right to determine whether the safety and fate of your children is in the right hands.

I will not go into the details of why 9/11 happened because it will not remain a letter but will become a book. I will therefore restrict myself to what happened after 9/11 and how your leaders acted on these crises. I have written a small book, "Terrorism or Awakening", which you may like to read in your leisure time to give you some idea of why I believe 9/11 happened. I, being an average man in the street myself, would like to address my similar American colleagues to at least reach somewhere close to the depth of these crises, the remedy adopted by your leaders and its long term effect on you, the real people.

9/11 was a huge tragedy not only because of the loss of lives and economy, but also the loss of prestige and honor. The entire world was sympathetic and became partners in grief and pain. The people's concern from all over the world, without any exception, should have been indeed regarded as a compensation and counter balance effect against this criminal offense committed by whom so ever. A big nation like you should have great moral courage to bear such loss and react coolly and with a great sense of wisdom and prudence. There was no reason to be jittery and react like a vagabond and get into serious perpetual trouble. Mind you, your getting into charade means trouble for the whole world. Your leadership should have the depth to bear the shock and not pass on the shock to others.

Mr. Bush's reaction to 9/11 was like a man in the street and not like someone sitting on the high platform, watching and protecting the United States of America. Even if it was an attack on America, it should have been dealt with proper planning and execution to nip the evil in the bud, instead of chasing a small group of riff raffs throughout the world. He behaved like a cowboy of the Wild West who believed in quick revenge from the rival group and spread fear amongst the people. You are now a leader of the world and therefore must maintain the honor of this status, lest someone snatches it from you. History has seen many such downfalls due to the follies of the incompetent leaders.

After 9/11, the first casualty was Afghanistan, the poorest in the world and governed peacefully by popular Taliban. One could differ with the way they were running the country but you could not deny their equity and virtue where people voluntarily joined them to save themselves from the cruel warlords and feudals. Their association with Osama Bin Laden was negotiable and could have been settled amicably with patience. The world would not have fallen for a few days. We would have saved ourselves from the catastrophe Mr. Bush and his associates caused in the entire region. Your alliance with the Northern Afghans, who were nothing but warlords and feudals, was indeed against your own belief and principle. With their collusion, you destroyed Afghanistan with Daisy Cutter and laser guided bombs and established "Guantanamo Bay," where hundreds and thousands of innocent people were brought and detained as suspected members of Al-Qaeda. You tarnished your own hundreds of years old justice system and got it in disrepute in the whole world. Barring ten odd detainees, the rest were proved innocent. Who will compensate them for the torture they underwent for years.

At least fifty thousand Afghan men, women, and children were killed in that senseless war. You also forced the President of Pakistan, Gen. Musharaf, to join and support this unjust war at a point of the bayonet. The Pakistani dictator, under duress, joined you in a so-called "war of terror". As a result, the Americans who were liked in Pakistan are now a symbol of hatred by the masses and the entire region is in the grip of instability and turmoil. Afghanistan by itself is in no better condition after five years of war. Your agent, Mr. Karzai, is as impotent today as he was during his installation as president. Democracy has gone further away and your honor even farther than this.

The second victim was Iraq. It is a point to ponder for all Americans what have they gained in the whole episode. Everyone in this region and beyond understands, except Americans, that the whole game to remove Saddam was to favor Israel. At least one hundred thousand Iraqis have been killed and a prosperous country destroyed for the sake of security of a small rogue country, Israel. The divide of Shia-Sunni and Kurd, created by you is an artificial phenomenon and shall vanish as soon as you leave which may be after a hundred years. It is in the knowledge of all saner elements in Iraq and they will not let Iraq be divided and disintegrated. I was in Iraq during Bath Party Revolution in 1968 and never learned of any such divide. Neither was any such philosophy prevalent before that revolution. I was there for almost three years and I observed no Shia-Sunni rift throughout. There was some unrest of the Kurds in the Northern area, which was basically initiated by Iran because of the Iran-Iraq political issue like Shatt-ul-Arab and other border disputes.

Democracy is not a medicine that you force down the throat of people at night and next morning they are democrat. It is a process of years education and behavior that ultimately put people on the right track. Today with the force of occupation you feel happy with election and its results. Tomorrow with occupation forces gone, democracy will also follow you to America and England. Iraqi's are not yet made for democracy. Your agent Mr. Zalmay Khalilzad cannot provide you credible advice or information to the stability of Iraq. There were some very respected and honorable people who could have saved the situation; if they were still alive. Find a reasonable plan to quit and put an end to such a senseless killing of Iraqi's and your own people.

Israel is a bone of contention between America and most of the Middle East countries that happen to be Muslim. In a broader sense, the cause of evil between the Muslim world and American leadership is Israel. American leadership has repeatedly demonstrated unfair judgment whenever it came to a decision between Arabs and Israel. Palestinians have suffered a great deal from Israel with intentional support from U.S leadership. It is commonly apprehended that the American Jews fully support Israel and since Jews in America are filthy rich, all political leadership needs money to fight election and win. They are forced to follow Jews just or unjust demands in lieu of political support from them.

I wonder if the American Jews understand that they are prosperous and rich because of America and not so much due to their own ability. If the Base diminishes, you fall on your face. So, be American and take off the garb of Israel. It will be good for Israel also to shed away the artificial legs and stand on their own. That will surely bring them closer to their neighbors.

The American leadership's desire to install Israel as a sheriff in the Middle East has proved counterproductive. I hope one day it does not harm America because America is a hope for the entire world. Haven't you learned a lesson from Soviets who wanted to do the same with Cuba in South America, so far from their country? You are committing the same folly in the Middle East. Soviets were poor and fell quickly. You are rich; you will take your own time. End result may be the same.

Now you have President Chavez of Venezuela at hand. Be good to him and his people. You may need them one day. Don't let your bad pedigree leaders destroy your future, the future of your children and their offshoots. Open your eyes and force them to change. Create love; not hatred.

We, in third world countries feel that the common man in America is like a "robot"—gets up in the morning, works throughout the day, reaches home exhausted after hours of commute, has a drink or two, eats, and sleeps. Repeat the same next day and after. He has no time to think and feel about what is happening to the poor of the world who has no money to drink. He eats sometimes and goes without it most of the times.

Sermons of your leaders for their actions, to strengthen your home security are a farce. Your security lies in making friends around the world, not creating enemies. Today, 90% of the third world countries people dislike America. That is a point to ponder.

Enough is Enough—Wrap up the End Sensibly

24th May 2007

Gen. Musharaf has been the eye of the storm in Pakistan environments for almost eight long years. For some he had been the angel who carried Pakistan safely through a very troubled period of history. Certainly he has been an angel of fortune for Ch. Shujahat, Shoukat Aziz, Mushahid Husain and Perez Ilahi who must thank Tariq Aziz for bringing this angel around them from Heavens. For a few old superstitions who believed in the stories of old grannies inspiring small children with stories of one eyed **giant** appearing out of lightning bringing hailstorm and terror, till a human sacrifice offered to secure relief and protection. Nawaz Sharif, Shehbaz Sharif and Benazir maybe some effected from such hazardous phenomenon, related by old grannies. However only history will prove whether, the General was an angel of rain and pleasantry or a one eyed **giant** bringing hailstone and fireballs.

The recent frustrations have forced the nation to review and re-evaluate all the events of the past eight years to ascertain "KIA KHOYA KIA PAYA." (What all we lost and what were the gains). After all history also has an element of speculation, major portion of which pertains to the prophecies and predictions.

National morale is a very delicate matter. It makes or breaks the nation in times of crisis. High morale is an asset that mobilizes the people towards progress and ascendancy while poor moral slides her down towards failure and misery. Whether we accept it or not, right now we are in crisis and unfortunately **Gen. Musharaf** is solely responsible for this. He is two in one (Army Chief and the President) and all in all in everything that effects the nation. All other Govt. machinery moves only, on his orders and whims. Another serious problem is the rumors that are affecting every individual today. When the rulers commit follies, they try to retrieve through all kinds of excuses and lies. Rumors at this stage are very damaging and should be arrested in time and strangled through facts and figures lest they destroy the national morale. There is no doubt and exaggeration that the country is under the grip of rumors and people are running around to find the fact and truth.

Basically the crisis started with one man, **Gen. Pervez Musharaf** and his appointment as the chief of army staff—by Prime Minister **Nawaz Sharif**. Although he promoted him out of turn. Yet the General somehow alienated himself from the Prime Minister for the reason well known to him. From the very outset it appeared that he was reluctant to subordinate himself to the civilian Govt. His first action to demonstrate an intentional defiance was to greet India's Prime Minister, Vajpayee when he came by bus to Lahore. This certainly caused anxiety to Mr. Nawaz Sharif that his authority was compromised by his own Army chief.

The second blunder was **Kargil** operation which was planned and executed by the Army without taking any consent and approval of the Govt. This was the most ill-conceived idea by any military general so far in Pakistan. After East Pakistan this was another humiliating defeat in the hands of Indians where we lost about 1000 gallant officers and men in this useless futile exercise. Politically the entire world attached the dogma of a rogue Army to our Arm forces. We lost our respect in the community of nations and our prime minister had to almost beg **Mr. Clinton** to rescue Pakistan from this embarrassing situation, and Pakistan army from this immoral and sinister status. Did we learn any lesson from this? We only resorted to "blame game" and left everything to time healing and once again hood winked the nation. However time also is very cruel and does not easily forgive without penalty to those who misuse it. We should have had a critical analysis of the operation and punish those responsible for it. We don't entrust the country and army to a few elected and selected people to merely enjoy the command and charm attached to it but also keep the rights to punish when they cause humiliation and indignity to the people of this country. Even today an independent inquiry is desired to secure the country from any future adventure like this.

Another blunder that many people are not aware was committed by him when as a Chief Executive; he deprived Pakistan Air Force from four very capable incumbents as chief of the Air staff appointment just because they did not support him on **Kargil** operation. This was literally crippling PAF at that time from the hard core experience, and competence. Although time provided the relief to preserve the ingenuity of the PAF, yet the loss of experience was damaging to PAF at that time.

Then came **12ᵗʰ Oct 1999**, when a very popular elected Govt. was overthrown and constitution abrogated for personal interest and as chief of army staff, using army to take over the country against all constitutional prohibitions. Subsequently forcing the legal president to quit and manipulating the judiciary to install himself as the president of Pakistan in uniform. Irrespective of his all circumvention, he was at that time guilty of being chargeable under **article 6** of the constitution. The drama of hijacking was as absurd as was the seven point agenda of running the country under illegitimate rule. Some of the political parties were also guilty of misconduct during this coup. Their behavior was no less culpable in the national politics.

Another apparently cunning and willful defiance to flout his own agreement with **MMA** to take off the uniform on **31Dec 2004** showed his very serious weakness of personal character. Irrespective of all other options he personally pledged on television to the entire nation that he shall take off the uniform on the above agreed date. He failed to do that on some pretext, which is not a subject matter here. However this was his personal commitment and if it was **not to be**, he should have then come back to the nation to justify his refusal to do so.

9/11 had one of the most detrimental effects on our well established civilized traditions of society. Our leader and **chief executive** behaved like a scared goat that ran whichever way he thought he could find safety for himself, with pretence to save Pakistan. This was the poorest display of character to destroy your brothers for your own security and protection. Taliban were the most loyal and faithful friends of Pakistan. They had done nothing to expect this hostile treatment from Pakistan. Quite a lot has already been said about this operation, adding more would be like burning our own hearts and the hearts of Afghans. Although it is against all values but if at all our chief executive decided to sell Pakistan, he should have sold it for at least 300 billion dollars and not for mere 3 billion. This disgraceful deal literally brought the nation in a state of surrender to a super power, America and I feel we are still under constant captivity of USA.

Dr. Abdul Qadeer Khan was the other victim of our **General** who humiliated him in front of the whole world. I am sure the brave and self respecting nations must be viewing us contemptuously, especially **India** who had elevated our hero's contemporary, Dr Abdul Kalam to president of their country.

The Americans will not forgive the general so easily. They promised to pay 3 billion dollars. They thought the price was enough to use Pakistan army to kill all friends of Taliban and those who looked like them in **North** and **South Waziristan**. It was not their problem if these people were our kith and kin. They also wanted some to be handed over to them for onward dispatch to Guantanamo Bay. To disgrace us further they promised to pay extra for this, because it was not included in the original deal.

The **General** also attacked Kashmir with a brigade of options to facilitate India to have complete control over Kashmir in due course of time. It is important to note that the present Azad Kashmir was taken by force by the Mujahideen in 1947. Pak Army assistance reached much later. It is pity that the children of those vary Mujahedeen are being declared as terrorist and massacred by Pak army. Some of them are being sold to Americans now as fuel and firewood for the Guantanamo Bay bonfire.

The **General** also promised to strike opposition leaders and so called terrorists in **Baluchistan** with such precision and secrecy that they would not know from where they were being hit. He proved that by killing **Akbar Bugti** and we are all still licking the wounds of that operation.

The last assault was on the **Chief Justice** of the Supreme Court of Pakistan. The president must know that no one believes the stories coming out of Govt. circle; he should therefore avoid convincing general public to accept the lies. If he can rectify the situation through courage and truth he should do that, otherwise silence is **'virtue'**.

Since most of the above have already been regularized through L.F.O. and 17th amendment, I as a veteran and as such well wisher of the

17

president, pray that, as a way out, an Interim National Government, acceptable to all parties be formed immediately with a view to work out modalities to smoothly transition into fully representative credible system of the government, which should meet the aspirations of all segments of the society; **How about wrapping up the End sensibly.**

An Open Letter to Iraqis

FOR GOD'S SAKE STOP KILLING EACH OTHER

14th Aug 2008

Iraq is in the grip of a civil war. There are three different forces pulling her in different directions. American and British like to steer her towards disintegration for easy control and dominance for all time to come. Israel wants it to be economically crippled, unable to equip herself militarily to challenge their authority in the region. America largely being a superstitious nation believes in **Nostradamus** prediction that some Muslim ruler in this area will rise and defeat the non believers and gain command of the world. They therefore were trying to stop that and are now generating hatred amongst the people of the region so that they never become a nation. Iraqis, of course want to come back to the path of peace, prosperity and progress. They want to defeat all those forces who are forbidding them to become a nation again.

Let bygone be bygone. You seem to have come out of all the trouble and setback. You need to evaluate things in the present perspective and reality. Unity is your only choice, grab it or else you may get scattered forever.

To me personally Iraq is like Pakistan. I take this opportunity to address my Iraqi brothers and express my feelings in retrospect when I served in Iraqi Air Force for almost three years.

Baghdad was my dream city. I spent some golden days of my life there. I made very good and life time friends and tried to keep contacts with them for as long as it was possible, but now I shudder to think about them for the reasons I cannot dare to mention. While leaving Baghdad I promised with them that I shall be standing with them to protect Iraq whenever that time came. I am indeed ashamed that I could not fulfill that promise. However I must tell them through this letter that my intentions are still the same and it will be an honor for me to sacrifice for Iraq.

A contingent of 11 Pakistan Air Force officers landed at Baghdad airport on the 6th of April 1968, on deputation to Iraqi Air Force. We were received by Iraqi Ministry of Defense and after usual arrival formalities taken to Hotel Tigress Palace in the heart of the city. The Hotel was located on the river Tigress. It was a small hotel and I think half of it was requisitioned by the Ministry of Defense for official guests. The entrance was opening towards Shahrah Rashid, most probably on the name of **Khalifa Haroon Rashid**. This road was the main business centre of Baghdad City. On the back, a terrace leading to the river. The evenings reminded us about the tales of fairies landing at night to play on a very mild tune of Arabic music. A few Russian families and local Iraqi crowd used to make it a civilized romantic place every evening.

Law and order situation was exemplary, better than any other civilized country of the world. People in the street were friendly, sympathetic and very courteous. It indeed presented an ideal place for living. If there were no restrictions I would have opted to spend rest of my life in Iraq

Besides some civilians I had some excellent friends in the Air Force. They included Air Force Chief **General Husain Hayavi**, Air Defense Commander **General Naama Delaimi, and Brigadier Qusai-Al-Fazli**. A very good friend **Colonel (R) Munder Vendavi**, who was a political contemporary of Saddam Hussain. Because of his political ambitions he was later sent by Saddam as Iraqi Ambassador to Romania, Japan, France and many other countries, never to return to Iraq. He resigned as Ambassador to Holland when Saddam attacked Kuwait. He was an excellent friend and a nationalist who loved Iraq more than any person of the ruling Junta.

There was never a dispute between Shia and Sunnis on any issue. What to talk of disputes there were no open differences between any communities in matters of religious, political or social affairs. In the place of work we never knew or heard of any divide between any sect or minority. We were totally unaware of who was who. All were Iraqis and nothing else. Even the differences between Iraq and Iran were not on sectarian but territorial issues. Iranians were free to visit Iraq on pilgrimage to Karbala, Najaf, Samarra and Baghdad. Common Iraqis considered them as welcome guests to Iraq. Our Iraqi friends frequently invited us to visit Karbala to see Iranian people.

The Bath party revolution occurred in July 1968. **General Ahmad Hassan Al Baqar** took over as head of state. It was almost a bloodless coup. Bath party was a pure secular party and consisted of Shia, Sunni and Christian elements alike. No one ever talked or heard of any religious discrimination or differences at any forum. Similarly when **Saddam Husain** took over in 1979 no one ever called himself Shia, Sunni or Christian. When Iraq invaded Iran more than half of Army consisted of Shia's and they fought with Shia Iran as Iraqis, not as sectarian elements of Iraqi Army. During the war Iraqi Shia casualties were almost in the same proportion.

Saddam was a very progressive man. During the Iranian war and after he carried out enormous developments in Iraq. They were not arranged or planned in accordance with the sectarian divide. Maximum developments were done in **Karbala, Najaf, Samarra** and **Basra** areas, all Shia populated sectors. The only Sunni majority area was Baghdad itself. It will be surprising to note that the minimum share was provided to Takrit area, his own home base. Even in Kurdish areas like **Kirkuk** and **Mosul** were given good attention as other important sectors of the country. It goes without saying that Saddam's main emphasis was Iraq as a whole.

During first Gulf War the Iraqi Army was equally manned by Shia and Sunni. There were no sectarian divide and everybody was treated as Iraqis. In the face of defeat some seeds of dissention were sown with Shias in the south and Kurds in the north and a revolt was maneuvered by the American invaders. However soon after the war a fresh appraisal of Saddam by American drove them to betray both Shia and Kurds and Saddam was indirectly directed to curb this revolt in his own way. He broke loose on both Kurds and Shias and inflicted grave atrocities as punishment for committing treason against their own government in collusion with the enemy.

After the revolt was quelled and routine prevailed in the entire country, some smell of bad behavior by Shias and Kurds polluted the normal way of life as was prevalent in the country before the 1ST Gulf war. This was indeed the first sectarian disease commencing in Iraq.

After defeat in the 2nd Gulf war and Saddam's expulsion, the general public in Iraq displayed a sign of unity and welcomed the ouster of Saddam but at the same time lamented aggression on their country and condemned it outright. This was not easily digestible by Americans and British. They regenerated the germs of sectarianism for the purpose of divide and rule. They aired the Shia Sunni dissentions and tried to separate Kurds as a separate entity and lure them as allies. Secondly in their view a separate Kurdish state will be a perpetual source of trouble in the area for Iraq, Iran, Turkey and Syria.

The emergence **of Muqtada Al-Sadre** and **Mullah Sustani** as Shia separatist in the south and southwest, Kurds in the north, was a deep Anglo-American conspiracy to divide Iraq in splinter groups and keep a week Sunni state in the centre, to ensure that Iraq never remain a strong country for all time to come. To give it a practical shape they contemplated a vision of deep hatred amongst all the three communities so that a voice of disunity and permanent divorce becomes a reality from where coming back would be impossible. To do this, they infiltrated at least thirteen thousand Israeli, MI6, CIA agents to plan and execute sectarian killing at all sacred places of these communities. Seventy to one hundred Iraqis per day were the victims of their planning accepting five to ten percent of their own losses. So far 670000 Iraqis have been murdered and almost 3 to 4 thousand of their own troops.

Saddam Husain was a dictator, but was Iraqi and a patriot. He never thought in terms of Shia and Sunni. He got maximum Kurds killed fighting against the government in the northern Iraq. Kurds were all Sunnis. If he ever discriminated between Shia and Sunnis he would have never indulged in the massacre of Kurds. He eliminated everybody who, he thought was an impediment in the progress of Iraq, irrespective of his sect or creed. Because of his dictatorial use of power he committed lots of successes on personal liberties of the people for which he has been punished. However he was an architect of Iraq's development and recognition as a power to be reckoned by the super powers. Shia and Sunni divide was not Saddam's trait and he never wanted this unholy treat between Muslims of different sects.

Iraqis therefore should never become a tool in the hands of invaders to kill each other and destroy Iraq's unity and her strategic position in the community of nations. The principle of, "united you rise and divided you fall" must be your motto. Democracy does not divide people into splinter groups but unite the country as a single strong entity to serve for the progress and development of all the people of the country. **So please stop killing each other as Shia, Sunni or Kurds but promote love and affection and make your country strong and civilized to match your ancient civilization which indeed had a leading position of Iraq in the world of that time**

Uncertainty gripping Pakistan

19ᵗʰ July 2007

Pakistan is burning and many countries around the world maybe enjoying the fireworks created by the rulers of Pakistan to entertain them. The Indians must be on top of the world to watch this fun. The Americans carefully examining how their plans are taking shape in breaking up this unfortunate country for their own advantage and the advantage of their strategic partners. Only a few friends of Pakistan (if some are still left), must be worried to this scene of disintegration of their friend who had tremendous potential to play an important role in the world politics, specially the Muslim world. Chinese must indeed be worried to see their faithful friend, the people of Pakistan on their way to ruination. Saudi's must be disturbed but unfortunately are not in a position to save a brother because the spirit that is behind all this operation may well be warning Saudis to stay away from all this.

The way things are going Pakistan is brought to stand at the edge and we all know that anything poised to such a predicament is in a very difficult situation. The man responsible for bringing the country to such a state must sensibly retract from this visible danger before we reach the point of no return. After all the army withdraws under heavy odds from a battle front. It is considered a retreat not a defeat. This is our own country, our own future; we must work for its survival without having any consideration for our personal ego. General Musharaf committed a folly to stage an unnecessary and needless coup to topple a well established democracy in Oct, 1999. Since then the country started slowly and slowly drifting towards deterioration. The so called economic development claimed by the military regime was nothing but a MIRAGE. Economic progress cannot come without the political stability and unfortunately we are politically a bizarre country today. Whatever money that we earned through killing our own people and people of our brotherly country, Afghanistan may soon disappear. This also includes the money that we earned through selling our mujahedeen to American friends as a raw material to Guantanamo Bay furnaces, is also about to drain out from national wealth. Some has already filled the few private pockets. We are gradually coming back to our original standing.

Pakistan is a dream country blessed with unlimited mineral resources. Mountains and rivers add to the beauty, charm and potential development opportunities. Above all the unmatched man power which is second to none in the world. It is so critically situated that no big and important country could afford to bypass her in any affairs of this region. It is indeed a bridge between China, Russia, East Asian states and West Asia. No country in the area can fully exploit her resources and take advantage of each other without crossing this vital bridge.

A dictator is undoubtedly the weakest link in a nation. This was one of the reasons General Musharaf was caught by the neck after 9/11 to join the Bush club and do what is told to him. This was accepted by him and we are victim of that subjugation till today. The general immediately put a tag of terrorist on most of the bearded Pakistanis. Supported American aggression on Afghanistan and provided all the required air bases and ground support facilities to assist Americans and their allies to consolidate the occupation of Afghanistan. Once you submit to a super power you have no choice to defy any orders passed by them. In the due course of time they thought that only support operations for Afghanistan were not enough, it has to be extended to Pakistan Afghan border to stop any infiltration of Taliban/mujahedeen allegedly supporting rebel Afghans against the allied forces. The General suddenly discovered that hundreds of terrorists and foreign insurgents were living in Pakistan side of the afghan border. An immediate operation involving 70,000 PAK troops were ordered to clear the area from these insurgents. An unfortunate open war was induced in which about one thousand Pakistani troops and hundreds of civilians were killed to fulfill the desires of the super power. However, the American's do more philosophy was stretching like a magic rope and the General was trapped to follow the rope willingly or unwillingly. Mr. Bush wanted the money's worth results and whatever damage done so far was not considered compatible to the price paid.

The General led us to an unending war which ultimately Afghans or Taliban are going to win. At least that is what history tells us. The allies are quietly going to pull out like they have done in the past in Vietnam, Cambodia, and Korea and would be contented at this fate accompli also. Pakistan will be the only loser in this entire sequence of events. We have already lost the national unity; look at Baluchistan, NWFP tribal belt and Sindh, especially Karachi. On the behest of the Americans, the General eliminated all supporting elements of Jihadist in Kashmir and declared numerous options to please India for a lasting peace. His prayers were totally ignored by the Indian government. He is still waiting some angel's echo to convince and pacify the nation. However, Indians are shrewd enough to continue striking while the iron is hot. On the other side General has no mandate from the nation to strike a bargain on Kashmir. He is, unfortunately again over estimating his personal judgment and over playing his genius like taking the ugly decision after 9/11.

Extremism is another creation of General Musharaf in Pakistan. Every nation and country has some element of extremists. Americans have many fanatics who every now and then kill quite a number of children in the schools or people in the market or bomb Oklahoma City. British have been fighting them for over fifty years. French, Italian and Germans are not free from them. Why is General Musharaf so anxious to provoke and irritate such elements to revolt and disturb our peace to suit Mr. Bush's plan of chaos and disturbance in this part of the world. Why should Pakistan take her sleeping GENIE out of the bottle? Whenever you create a monster it is bound to come after you at the end of the day. This is exactly what happened at Jamia Hafza and now in the Tribal belt of NWFP. Whatever short fall to create further instability in the country was filled up through a totally mala-fide reference of the chief justice of the Supreme Court which is indeed adding fuel to the fire already ablaze in the country.

The general must step aside to save himself and the country. Let people of Pakistan deal with the monster he has created. I hope he gets a divine courage to retrieve from the follies that he has committed to bring the country to this state. Let the exiled leadership return to Pakistan and lead their parties in a free and fair election and bring the country back on track. May god help the people of Pakistan in this critical, decisive and gripping moment.

Benazir (BB) & The General

18ᵗʰ August 2007

The generals in Pakistan have a knack of catching politicians by the tails and then play with them at their own will. It was astonishing to see BB, out of all the people falling into the trap. It is not yet clear what kind of booby trap had General laid down to catch a big fish like Benazir Bhutto. We all thought BB had a very sensitive tail and it was not for any General's ability to have an access to it. For some school of thought it could be other way around that this time the General's tail was in her hand. But the Army still being with the General, it upholds to a Punjabi proverb that; "CHUREE KHARBOZA KAY NEECHAY HO YA UPER; KOI FARAK NAHI PARTA" (Whether the knife is under or over the melon, it is all the same). However, the whole nation is watching very critically who will be the victim of the trap and fall in the ditch this time.

General Zia-ul-Haq is considered the cleverest of all his counterparts coming before or after him. He was indeed a General and a politician also. Even Americans had to accept this and get rid of him in the end. Politicians were his special subjects. He, in his personal thesis pronounced that he had to only give a hint and almost all politicians would come running wagging their tails and sit down before him like a faithful animal. Musharaf is not as clever, but General is a General, he follows the SOP (standard operating procedure) of his old Bosses. Unfortunately he could not apply this formula on most of the politicians but at least caught one and that also a big one. I am again taking cover of an old Punjabi proverb that "Only the most intelligent crow chooses to fall in the trap".

How the whole thing has come about is anybody's guess. The General is still in uniform and is negotiating with the same skin that he had achieved before deliberations. BB on the other hand was insisting that he removes his skin before she could sit with him. She had indeed laid down tough conditions to negotiate. The beauty of the negotiation is, to proceed sentence by sentence and to move point by point to reach the goal. Sometimes one party could reckon to achieve something when the other retrieves from the firm position a little, to keep the proceedings alive. It appears that the General has successfully advanced in the battlefield. If he can hold his position he would be regarded to come as close or near the sight of victory. However, the time will tell whether the General can hold the position or BB forces him to retreat.

The General in his previous speeches and conferences always blamed BB and her husband, Mr. Zardari as the most corrupt politicians and government of Pakistan had charged them with no. of national and international lawsuits against them. He explicitly declared in public meetings that she would not be allowed to come back and take part in the fourth coming elections unless she cleared her corruption charges both national and international. What has changed now? Has she been absolved of all the charges or else the General has found the ladder to reach her level and both are now identical, in the same robe to rule this unfortunate nation.

The Americans are sitting at the apex with a string to move things in their own way. They don't want any interference in the Afghan operations. At present they cannot find a better replacement of Gen. Musharaf. Democracy in Pakistan is neither their aim nor choice. Unfortunately the General has been lately committing follies after follies and has become unpopular. That is their main irritant at present. They want to supplement him with another popular public figure, which they have been grooming for a long time. The time of implementation has come whether the General likes it or not. Both have been directed to tolerate each other under the circumstances, for their own survival.

In Pakistan Muslim extremists and terrorists are continuously causing distress to Mr. Bush, and he has to task his own faithful to deal with them. There seems no better and suitable time to test his long term protégées. Despite their personal likes and dislikes, the General and BB have to accept each other to demonstrate their loyalties to the Americans. BB needs position and authority in Pakistan. The Americans are ready to help but she has to share with the General. BB tried to have her own way but it did not work out. She had to accept whatever was available. The power hungry politicians have no principles and they crave for the power and position no matter how it comes. Robert Novak, in his memoirs has rightly said, "They are all disappointing because they are just politicians. The only perfect man was Jesus Christ and he never ran for any position".

The question arises that if she was bargaining with Musharaf then why was she impatient to sign the charter of democracy with Nawaz Sharif and Party. Her party now says that she is a politician and she has to do a lot of things for public consumption. Truth and honesty is not name of the game in politics. These are only left for Nawaz Sharif, Qazi Hussain Ahmad and Imran Khan who have yet to do their homework and pass the test in politics. The same thing she repeated in the APC (all parties' conference), where, though she did not participate but her party was in forefront and all the top party leaders committed in public to fight for democracy and ouster Musharaf and Army from the politics. How those leaders would be compromising with their conscience and come to terms with themselves. They must either be feeling frustrated or connived by their chairperson for this betrayal at national level.

The superpower tends to take advantage of the weakness of poor countries or its greedy leaders and use them as trump cards at an appropriate time. This happens every day and repeated as necessitated by a political situation. BB has to live in Abu Dhabi and off and on visit America and Europe to manage her personal accounts. This is her compulsion. The other prominent party leaders have to endorse her point of view to align with General Musharaf under duress.

Cheer Iraq

(The destruction of Iraq is in no one's interest)

18ᵗʰ August 2007

I am no Nostradamus but I can see very clearly written on the horizon that Iraq is coming back; Back to its old glory by shearing off the shackles of slavery from the Anglo-American occupation. The defeat had provoked the people to pickup an eccentric behaviour and the blame game which had divided them into Sectarian and other regional groupings. It had totally demolished them to recognize the relationship and bond between each other, killing thousands of their comrades without any rationale. It is indeed a madness which has to be redressed. However, the time is bringing the sanity back into them and they are beginning to realize that unity is their only choice to save them from getting into a nameless future. They are trying to pull their heads up their shoulders to see things clearly beyond their feet. Hopefully they are able to sit together and sort out the differences and join to, firstly steer themselves out of the occupation, and secondly to put themselves back on track to progress and prosperity. They have enough resources to rebuild the country again without any outside help. The invaders also have an obligation, to assist because the destruction was their mission and therefore rehabilitation should also be their responsibility.

The Anglo-American alliance is probably very keen to breakup Iraq into three small states comprising of Shia, Sunni and Kurdish areas as a long term colonies like tiny African states. To them Iraq as a single unit is the only Arab country that upsets their future plans for the Middle East. They want to incapacitate Iraq for any future clash with Israel. Secondly to use her oil resources without any challenge for all times to come. I cannot help saying 'Man proposes but God disposes'. If wishes were the horses everyone would ride on them. On the other side Iraqis must know that their strength and survival lies only in their unity. They certainly would not like to be another Abu Dhabi or Qatar.

It is indeed very unfortunate that the Americans are averse making friends with Muslims in the area. They only prefer slaves and not friends because friends are partners and hold their own distinct opinion for mutual respect and benefits. One way traffic in human relations is not acceptable. All Arabs including Iraq want to have a fair and judicious treatment between Israel and themselves. They resent having inequity between Israel and Arabs. Unfortunately Americans are bent upon using their Veto in favour of Israel even if it amounted to lose their respect and name in the community of nations in the world. How on earth can then Americans and self respecting Arabs meet, each following the parallel lines. However, history has it's own course that follows without any time constraint. No super power stays forever. The Romans, Greeks, and Persians have perished. The Muslims faded away, and the Russians have vanished. Who knows what lies ahead for our American friends. Only the name is immortal and you cannot achieve this status with Guantanamo Bay and Abu-Gharaib performance. You need to come to terms with justice to save your name.

Iraq has been the hub of civilization and a mini super power in a distant past. It has a history far superior to that of America. It therefore needs a respect that it deserves. The people had their way of living that cannot be easily forgotten and set aside. The new generation follows a history of the recent past which may be given a serious consideration while solving the current problems. The past hundred years are very fresh in the minds of a common man and the system they have followed in this course has become part of their life, as such a change not conforming to their nature, is resisted. Let us be honest and frank; Democracy at present is not their choice. It has been thrust upon by the invaders and is considered motive oriented. Acceptance has to come from within and not from outside and that also by force. They are used to be governed in a system that goes back to Prince Abdullah and Prime Minister Noorie-al-Syed, modified by Abdul Karim Qasim and further transformed by Abdus Salaam Arif followed by Saddam Hussein.

I am sure the Anglo-American Think Tanks must be busy finding a way to pull out. Iraq has become a Vietnam. Sooner or later it has to be vacated. The hoax of democracy has not worked. They have to come up with a better solution to clean up the mess they have created. The seeds of dissension are proving counterproductive. I think the destruction of Iraq as a country is in no one's interest. If the Iraqis are losing, you are not gaining either. It is too big a country to be completely knocked down. There has to be some compromise solution. At times you might have to negotiate with a devil to strike a deal, but it has to be a devil from within. Outside devil has not worked before and it is not going to work again. The ghost of Al Qaeda will not be able to make any dent if the Iraqis are willing to subscribe.

One obvious factor is your willingness to pull out of Iraq and declare an exact timetable to withdraw. This should produce a lightening effect on Iraqis and provide favourable sentiments towards Americans and British. The natural reaction would be to facilitate smooth and peaceful withdrawal activities to inspire confidence and mutual respect. A further announcement of aid package for reconstruction and leaving behind maximum of military equipment, brought during war, for the Iraqi forces will reduce the tension all around to help safe withdrawal of forces from different routes. After all, the massive strength of the Army would need to be evacuated through land routes to friendly countries like Jordan and Kuwait. The second most important affect would be Iraqis gathering their own intelligentsia and think tank to bring about National unity and respect for each other's point of view. Discourage warlords and religious leaders to interfere in the government's affairs to establish law and order. However, it is a difficult situation for them to create that harmony under the circumstances. It may take a long time to heal the wounds of hatred created by either the invaders or because of the result of the defeat.

A few more resolve may be possible but a surprise move has to be exercised at an appropriate moment for an effective result. Stability at any cost is vital and must be maintained.

Whatever the treatment, the healing process has already started. The British Army is fed up with casualties that are increasing every day. The American public is furious for the same reasons and are beginning to recall the horrendous days of Vietnam. All roads are leading to the same end that Iraq is coming back and it is time for all of us to provide a safe landing to them for the sake of world peace and stability of the region.

Hitler Re-born to destroy Lebanon

30th July2006

Hitler is part of world history and like history repeats itself, Hitler will keep coming back in our life and remind us about the good and bad effects of his era, as long as his spirit lives. We don't know or, shall we say we are not sure as yet whether the spirit is actually immortal and will always live or remain as long as the world exists. So is the case with other good and bad, believed to be immortal. Recent events in the world somehow pertain to similarity of actions taken by Hitler during the World War 2. We are therefore trying to bring back the memories of him and imply that these things maybe having some connection with the evil dealers of today committing sins towards their fellow beings. The weak have always been punished by the strong because they are incapable of retaliations or reacting in the same way to those by whom they are made to suffer. The strong evil also tries to incapacitate the weak to ensure that they remain in the same state of incapacitation for all times to come.

During World War 2, Hitler resorted to bombing the civilian targets and innocent people to bring about whatever he thought was right and necessary to achieve victory. The bombing of London was the most blatant case of treachery and destruction of civilian life and property not concerned in any way with the war. About thirteen and half thousand people were killed and eighteen thousand injured with at least twenty five thousand made homeless. Mr. Churchill retaliated with all the Might and avenged in the same manner by destroying the German cities of Dresden and Hamburg with much more casualties and damage. According to Nazi statistics about hundred and forty to two hundred fifty thousand people were killed and most of the city buildings were raised to the ground. One could justify the reprisal of Mr. Churchill, however, he cannot be totally absolved of the crime committed against innocent citizens who had nothing to do with the killing and destruction of English people. Hitler was nevertheless the cause of these atrocities and was rightly punished. His country and the poor innocent people merely suffered because of him. He was also guilty of Holocaust and cruelty to Jews. About 1.3 million Jews were killed. However, Jews claim to have lost five million out of which three million were Polish Jews.

The allies conquered Germany and divided it into different segments and occupied by all the parties concerned. The Jews ran away from Germany and were forced upon the Palestine by the American and European leaders. The purpose was to oblige them now and use them in times of any crisis in future conflicts between the west and the rest of the world. Although one can hardly predict the intentions but the intended plan has now been exposed by the history as settling the influx of Jews exodus to Palestine was nothing but a stab on the back of Palestinian Arabs. Hitler's treatment of Jews during Holocaust left tremendous effect on Jews behaviour and character. It went into their blood to behave like Hitler's way of dealing with the weak and oppressed. After settlement and establishing Israel they started treating Palestinian with the same method and technique they had acquired from German leadership and elite. About four to five million hard liner Palestinians were pushed from their homeland to different Arab countries. This indeed amounted to reincarnation of Hitler's spirit in modern Israeli Jews. I feel it is now up to these rejuvenated Jews to realize and change for good instead of following Hitlerian philosophy.

The recent escalation in Lebanon reflects the same expansionist designs adopted by Hitler in Europe and Russia. Although he had territorial hunger but his methodology was nothing but cruelty towards the civilian population. Israel has no capacity to expand but her oppressive treatment towards the weak is no less than Hitler's behaviour towards Jews. This insight streak of Hitler's characteristics speaks of their behaviour towards the people under their occupation and weak neighbours.

Two of Israeli soldiers captured by Hezbollah have brought about the destruction of half the Lebanon and her infrastructure. It is in no way justifiable under any rules. This was of course done because there was no fear of any reprisal from a weak country like Lebanon or any other impotent Arab neighbours. Likewise, Israel is holding unaccounted prisoners from Palestinians and Hezbollah. If this is the way to exchange prisoners, its legitimization should be cited in Geneva

Convention. Mr. Bush and Blair's sermon of self defence by Israel is indeed an encouragement and blessing to her for invading Lebanon. It is an immoral support and is difficult for the world to swallow. The world should wake up to save Lebanon from the atrocities committed by Israel, as was done to save the Jews from the clutches of Hitler. What a pity and world's helplessness to save poor civilian victims from the Israeli tyrants with Hitler's spirit working in their blood.

On 25th July 2006 it was very interesting to watch on BBC 1 about cruelty to animal and remedial actions to save these animals from the mistreatment. It was even suggested to take legal action against culprits responsible for this cruelty. Can we also do the same for the poor oppressed citizens of Lebanon being crucified by Israel due to Hitler's spirit still active in them. The unfortunate support by Mr. Bush and Brother Blair is no surprise to the world. Hitler also had the similar support from Mussolini of Italy and Japanese government.

UNO basically exists because of Americans and European donors, it therefore by and enlarge performs in their interest. It behaves like a poor spectator when it comes to observe excesses committed by the Americans and their ally Israel. It has time and again shown helplessness on all issues relating Israeli aggression against her neighbours. The support of democracy seems the main feather in her cap, yet it herself is devoid of this blessing. The power of veto is ample proof of the fact that the world organization is actually working on principle of **'might is right.'** The veto power at the Security Council is a weapon used most effectively by the super power against any adversary at will. Many problems and disputes like Kashmir, Palestine, Cyprus etc are still unresolved for the last so many years because of this anomaly of veto power.

The international court of justice has tried German leadership after World War 2, Mr. Milosevic and Saddam Hussein for human rights violations and war crimes. I wonder when they are going to try Mr. Bush, Tony Blair and Israeli leadership for having blood of thousands of Afghans, Iraqi, and Palestinian civilians on their hands. An Urdu poet Muneer Niazi has very rightly said, **'on whose hands can I find**

the blood of my murder; The entire city is wearing the gloves.' Let people of the world wake up and save Lebanon, put an end to the Hitler's incarnation in the shape of Israel and make this world a better place for us all to live.

Only God knows the Afghanistan Future

24ᵗʰ Aug 2007

25ᵗʰ Dec' 1979 was a shocking day for the ordinary Afghans who suddenly woke up by the roar of Russian tanks and lorry full of Russian soldiers along with the swarm of footed army marching on the streets of Kabul. It was like a bomb shell to those poor people who were completely ignorant of the political affairs of the country. Their eyes were opened with the morning announcements by their government radio that the Russians were invited to manage the deteriorated conditions and reform the country with the communist system to replace the prevailing the semi-Islamic rule. They regarded the existing system as outdated and primitive and totally against the interest of the poor. God or no God the country now will be governed by the communist doctrine. The Afghan government declared having invited the Russians to introduce these reforms to eliminate poverty from Afghanistan. The shock turned into an outrage and disturbance for the people who were beginning to realize the religious extinction. The Islamic belief and faith was so deep rooted that no other system could have made any dent in the heart of people.

Communism was known to be a godless society as such was completely unacceptable to the common man. There was obvious agitation which ended up in a revolt. The Russians were tough and insistent to their objective and they directed the local Afghan government and their own administrator machinery to use force if required to establish law and order in the country. Because of the fear of persecution the Afghan youth and some of the intelligential started fleeing to Pakistan and Iran. Pakistan being easily accessible and Pakhtoon populated on the border was more favourable for any future struggle against the soviets. The Russians were probably happy to get rid of the trouble makers who may never come back because of better prospects of living in Pakistan.

The people of Pakistan having strong bonds and religious faith in Islam welcomed the influx of Afghan brothers to shelter in Pakistan. I must mention here that it was not because of just the neighbourly relation but the Islamic faith is so strongly ingrained that any Muslim in trouble will readily be accepted and helped by the other Muslims to establish themselves. The world must understand that the Muslims world over are bound by this Islamic spirit that keeps them closer to each other like their own thick and thin. The west tried to exterminate these feelings during World War I and II but given then healing time it always came back with more vigour and affections. The western think tanks must not refrain from this background but face the facts because circumventing the reality is indeed away from it.

Most of the refugees' youth decided to fight the Russians and establish the force to commence Guerrilla warfare. Some educated and well known figures amongst them volunteered they organize the fight and lead the revolution. They were readily accepted by the majority and that is how the seeds of uprising were sown. The world is the witness what happened when the crop reached its harvest. The leaders responsible for this trouble were; Sibhatullah Mujededi, Burhanuddin Rabbani, Engineer Gulbadin Hikmatyar, Abdulrab Rasool Sayaf, Ahmad Shah Masood and at the end General Rasheen Dostum. The government of Pakistan provided all the facilities to organize the crowd into a disciplined force. An extensive training programme was arranged to train people in war tactics and use of modern weapons. Americans sitting on the hedge were watching all the activities critically to play their role as a super power. In that cold war era they wanted to engage the other superpower in a humiliating way and shatter her economically. The other more compelling reason was to revenge the defeat in Vietnam, where the soviets played the main role in defeating USA. It was in this background that Americans came in a big way with money and war material for the Afghan freedom fighters to put up a tough resistance and ultimately a decisive blow to the soviets like they arranged in Vietnam against Americans. In fact the Americans went a step ahead and provoked Muslim world to join Jihad against the soviets who committed aggression against an Islamic country. The Muslim freedom fighters from all over the world and especially from the Middle East started pouring into Pakistan to join their Afghan brothers to fight in Afghanistan.

Pakistan which was already acting as a conduit was delegated to act as headquarters and it's ISI (inter services intelligence) to manage and control the whole operations. USA provided all financial and material assistance which included the most modern weapons to fight. The ISI conducted training, developed plans and carried out all Guerrilla operations under their strict supervision. The strategy adopted by the ISI was so affective that it had tremendous demoralizing affect on the Russian troops because of the enormous army casualties, which also started telling its toll back home.

The Russians were beginning to retreat. The resistance of freedom fighters was so strong and resolute that they could not bear the pressure and burden of the war casualties, which resulted in total economic collapse. 1986 brought a complete collapse and Russian openly announced their retreat from Afghanistan.

There is no doubt that the afghan victory would not have been achieved in such a short time without the American assistance. However, it is absurd to imagine that it could not be possible without their participation and help. Probably it would have taken another ten years to succeed but victory had to come. Basically it is the will power, conviction and belief of the people who were ready to sacrifice their lives to beat the enemy out of their homes.

When the Russians started leaving there was a scramble by different groups of freedom fighters to grab the government seat and power to takeover. There were dissension between them and a new battle for the power started and almost all of them took up arms against each other. General Zia ul Haq, the then president of Pakistan and Saudi Arabia tried their best to settle them but failed. There was a complete anarchy where all groups made their own rule in the area under their control. A total chaos and law and order situation was completely nonexistent and so was the security. Looting, killing and rapes were the order of the day. Drugs and poppy production and smuggling were the main trade with the outer world. No one from within or without could keep a check on the affairs. The whole world, especially the West was in trouble because of the drug trafficking.

God knows Mullah Umar
Who is Karzai?

27ᵗʰ Aug 2007

After the Russian defeat in 1986, Afghanistan became a battle ground between the people themselves. All the warlords and the freedom fighters were virtually threatening to cut each other's throat to grab the power and takeover the government. General Zia ul Haq, the then president of Pakistan and the king of Saudi Arabia tried their best to mediate and establish peace but failed to reach any workable solution for sharing the power between them. The freedom fighters turned into law breakers and looting, killing and rapes became order of the day. The poor people became the victim of new masters amongst their own people. There was complete anarchy in the country and people became as insecure as they were during the Russian occupation.

The lawlessness increased to an extent of creating tension and agitation amongst the Afghan refugees in Pakistan and turmoil in Afghanistan itself thereby creating instability in the entire region. This was a distress signal not only for Pakistan but for the West and America to take notice of the coming danger of political upheaval and menace of drug trafficking all over the world. As it happened the poppy fields were blooming and drugs flourished as a main export item to be smuggled to the outside world.

After strict surveillance, all the stakeholders (Pakistan, USA, Britain, and Saudi Arabia), picked up Taliban to rectify this alarming situation. Mullah Umar, a very pious, truthful, and honourable man was assigned to takeover and coordinate with Talibans studying in Pakistan bordering areas and in Afghanistan to take up arms against the warlords. With the connivance of Pakistan and Saudi Arabia, he established a governing body in Kandahar, second big city South West of Kabul. He quickly got things under control and became very popular amongst the people. His dealings were so fair and just that the people voluntarily joined his ranks to fight against the warlords and evil doers. Within almost one and a half years, the Talibans swept through entire Afghanistan and established a firm control of the country by installing a central government in Kabul. The warlords became so scared of the people's strength that they voluntarily gave up their powers and surrendered to the government unconditionally.

By 1996 Taliban established a full working government in almost 90% of Afghanistan, barring a small portion of northern Afghanistan, which remained under the control of General Abdul Rasheed Dostum and Northern Alliance. People in general throughout the country hailed Taliban government and it was indeed like a democracy born without the elections. The first thing they established was the rule of law irrespective of the status of an individual. The second was the security of people and equal justice for all. The third very important thing was to eradicate all kind of drug trafficking from Afghanistan. However, from West point of view a few disagreeable factors were, their behaviour with women education and fraternizing with the foreign mujahedeen who had been fighting with Russians alongside Afghans, Al Qaeda and its boss, Osama Bin Laden; in particular; who were involved in a few anti American terrorist activities, in Kenya. According to the information available, no serious efforts were made to solicit with Taliban to negotiate with Al Qaeda to sort out the real bitterness between Al Qaeda and USA because a little while ago they were both friends in arms against the Soviets. I feel the bridge between them increased because of the authoritative behaviour of Americans to force their testaments on them. This was somehow not acceptable to Mullah Umar also who was neither ready to hand over his guest to Americans nor happy to expatriate him from Afghanistan against their own traditions. For this act of chivalry the Talibans had to pay such a big price tom endure the horrors of laser guided and daisy cutter bombs from the old friends. A little bit of perseverance in negotiations could have brought the situation under control and saved almost a million lives from both sides and enormous amount of money which could have been spent to eliminate poverty in the world over. After six years of killing and destruction you are now beginning to realize that negotiation with moderate Talibans is possible to bring peace and amity back. Political exigencies and a little patience could have saved both the parties from catastrophe they are in today.

One wonders today, where are those who fought for the liberation of Afghanistan from the Russians. Are they part of the present setup or they are hiding behind the curtain watching what has happened to the country for which their kith and kin laid down their lives and tolerated all sorts of torture, discomfort, pain and sufferings. Where is Sibghatullah Mujadedi, engineer Hikmat Yaar, Adul Rab Rasool Siaf, and their other comrades now?

Who is Hamid Karzai? From where has he surfaced to rule Afghanistan without shedding a drop of his blood for this poor country? Is it because he was lackey of the Northern Alliance and was ready to wash their dirty linen, or an American agent to serve their purpose. In fact he is neither of this. He is only slave of his ambitions and would betray anyone to realize his own dreams. How can one be trusted who does not subscribe even to his own motherland? He was elected as president under a fake and shame democracy, imported by the invaders, nurtured by the Northern Alliance and supported by general Musharaf, the president of Pakistan. The votes were either bought or imported through General Musharaf. The real sons of Afghanistan were not allowed to even come anywhere close to Kabul. However, the whole democracy and authority of Mr. Karzai is restricted to the city of Kabul only.

It is really not clear why the current exercise of so called liberation of Afghanistan was under taken by USA and UK. Was it only to benefit Mr. karzai? Or experimenting Waterloo for British and NATO troops. It indeed seems repetition of the CIA's conduct with small Latin American countries like Guatemala, Chilli, Bolivia, Nicaragua, Cuba, and Venezuela where the government after government was toppled on flimsy grounds. Americans gained nothing but ill-will and resentment of these small countries. Hugo Shavez of Venezuela, Micheue Bachelet of Chilli, and Nicanor Duarte Frutes of Paraguay are witness to all these exploitations which will not be so easily forgotten.

The American and British people whose tax payer's money is being wasted in Afghanistan and whose young soldiers are being killed, have to honestly analyze why their governments have indulged in this dangerous venture. Was it for the call of democracy or for saving Afghan women or to destroy Al Qaeda? If it was for the first two reasons, it was no one's business but the people of Afghanistan to change their lives. If it was to knock off Al Qaeda, there were many other ways to deal instead of going to the option of war and atrocities. However, having committed these follies will it be in the interest of their own people to continue or to stop this insanity? I am sure there are twenty ways other than the one of confrontation and war. We all hope the sanity prevails to stop bloodshed of your young soldiers and poor civilians and innocent children of Afghanistan.

In the light of recent history there is no one more experienced and qualified than the British to offer their genius to settle this issue. Mr. Bush and Party maybe more resourceful in providing support but UK's knowledge and skill of centuries in dealing with the people of this region has no match. Our prayers are with them to mentally and physically intervene to play the role of Jesus Christ to bring an end to this brutality. British cannot remain disconnected with the region because people of this area including Pakistan have played a great part in protecting their dignity and honour in both the World Wars. Most of the Indian Army came from this part which is now Pakistan. There are many from them now citizens of UK whose kith and kin are being killed in this senseless war. It is better to cement centuries old relations rather than demolish the deep rooted foundations just for a misconception of some and false ego of a few.

Talibans are none others than citizens as good as any other Afghans. They are not wrong in considering it their duty to oust the invaders as they did in case of Russians. Why talk of Islamic Jihad, even Jesus Christ leads you to a CROSS rather than living in luxury and grandeur.

How unfortunate that the British are now thinking of producing new enhanced blast weapons for using against Talibans. Instead of burning the old ones and adopting reconciliation they are trying to escalate the existing situation. Your own troops might be victim of these very weapons in future. After all the Talibans don't produce any weapons, the ones they are using now, are the product of the West.

The Americans have dragged Mullah Umar to Al Qaeda and Al Qaeda to half of the world. Taliban were a different entity and were restricted to Afghanistan only. Mullah Umar has so far never shown any affiliation with Al Qaeda except initially providing shelter to Osama Bin Laden in accordance with his traditions and cultural decorum. What other crime he had committed to move the entire West and NATO forces to trample his country, kill innocent women and children without any fault. The atrocities already committed by the Americans by dropping innumerable laser and daisy cutter bombs should be considered enough retribution for sheltering Osama Bin Laden.

Mullah Umar's character maybe judged through two American women journalist who were imprisoned by Taliban for spying; the women were so well treated that they accepted Islam on their return to USA and wrote a book on the whole incident of their stay in the prison. This may provide a fair comparison between a civilized prison of Guantanamo Bay and Abu Ghraib and an uncivilized extremist's prison in Afghanistan.

God knows Mullah Umar; who is Karzai and Bush to pass judgment on him.

A Deal, Disgraceful for All

31st August, 2007

Pakistan is nowadays in the grip of deals. General Musharaf and his team going to Dubai, Benazir running to America and Nawaz Sharif receiving delegates from Musharaf, are common topics of today. This entire struggle is to elect General Musharaf for next five years term as President. Everyday a new rumour is polluting the environments and creating tension all around. Background differs but the smell is the same. Gossip originators feel that they are moving in such secrecy that nobody has an air of it. How is it possible that the fire is without the smoke or the smell remains within the four walls? The smell leaks out of the door cracks/squeaks or from under the carpet. The rat-smellers have no other job but to keep themselves abreast with the situation, and then there is Media watch who is on the look out to approach their customers before somebody else does it.

The people are fed up with all these conspiracies and expect an honourable behaviour from their leaders, at least once for the sake of Pakistan. Musharaf wants to be elected for another five years in uniform with the promise to take it off after the elections. People don't trust him because he had gone back at his promise before. None other than his own party is willing to support him as both the Army Chief and the President. A few political leaders like to share the power and make a deal to oblige him. It is also believed that the General wants to exploit or blackmail the most prominent leaders, to stay in power. Benazir and Nawaz Sharif are two leaders heading the biggest parties of the country. Unfortunately both of them are living out of Pakistan, one on self exile and the other on forced exile on General's order.

General Musharaf is keen to have a deal with both or one of them, to suits his purpose. His team of solicitors are working hard on both the leaders to accept his terms to bail them out of their misconduct or charges and in lieu agree to their legitimate rights to return in the interest of the country. With all the regards for the ability of president's team to serve his purpose, I wish they had the courage to advise the president that it was time for him to go and not to extend the un-extendable period.

The General had, on many occasions in the public meetings and on television, accused Benazir as the most corrupt political leader charged with financial misappropriations within and out of the country. She is already under trial for this in the national and international courts of justice. She would not be allowed to fight the forth coming elections unless she cleared these charges. The deal with her signifies a breach of principles by the General and is totally against all moral ethics. Political Base stands on moral values and may never be violated under any circumstances, particularly from a person of president's stature especially when it serves his personal benefits. This will be considered dishonesty in performance of his duty and oath.

Benazir for a long time had been struggling to have some deal with the military regime with an excuse to provide Army, a way out from politics. She somehow never came anywhere close to Army's favour. She also tried to steal American favour but failed to achieve owing to American own relations with Musharaf because of the war against terror. However, she kept putting political pressure on Musharaf at his every weak moment. Charter of democracy with Nawaz Sharif was part of the same strategy. Her party support to Chief Justice of Supreme Court was also connected with the same. The recent events are ample proof of her planning and selfish designs for handling both to achieve her purpose of getting to power. One fails to understand why our politicians regard every wicked and unethical conduct as part of the real political manoeuvre. Is politics such a shameful profession that teaches you to seek power through any immoral means and make fool of innocent simple people supporting them for the sake of Pakistan.

Nawaz Sharif has so far been avoiding deals with Musharaf. Future is nobody's friend. Destiny decides despair and hopes on your behalf. Nawaz Sharif being from a religious background maybe strict believer of that, though it is not uncommon to change under stress or greed. Whatever future brings will be known to the people because hiding the truth is not possible, it comes out of the creeks and cracks of the walls. However, Musharaf needs a deal and he doesn't care from where it comes; Benazir or Nawaz Sharif.

General needs to comply with constitutional requirements because he says he has not ever gone against the constitution. This maybe either a joke or sense of humour which people are now quite familiar with.

The General needs deal to stay in power, and the Americans need General to protect their interest. Benazir is just a gap filler. The political support lost by the General through his own follies has to be covered up by Benazir, and the Americans are trying to arrange this marriage of inconvenience to suit their purpose. To make it look real some kind of show has to be presented for sharing power between both of them. There is of course nothing for Pakistan in the whole episode. If the General has come down to disregard all his utterances about Benazir and is ready to forgive her from all charges, people must have the sense to understand this practical joke.

The Americans interest is legitimate because of the war on terror where Musharaf is a partner and they don't like to change a faithful. The "Pakistan first" now demands that the author of it must honour his own words and accept the decision of the people irrespective of personal desires. The General forcing himself to stay with all pretence and cover-ups is making mockery of the slogan "Pakistan first" conceived by him. Making deals with all unwanted elements to remain in power does not suit his stature. He must accept that he failed the nation on many critical moments and crisis like 9/11, Kashmir, mala fide reference of Chief Justice and the last of all his personal and national elections. At least this is what, the nation pleads to the General to call it a day and save his name and honour of the nation.

Deals used in the sense of what is happening in Pakistan, are a nefarious activity and no person of integrity and honour should involve himself in this trash because the smell of it is bad and is polluting the whole country. This is not only true for the General but applies equally to any political leader accepting these for the purpose that the General is holding, is equally guilty of deceiving the nation. The people are on watch to observe affects of these deals on Pakistan's future and should make use of their choice in the coming National elections.

Guard Your Nuclear Assets

12ᵗʰ December 2007

End of emergency is about to be declared by Gen. Pervez Musharaf. In spite of this go Musharaf go is heard at every nook and corner of the country. Be-Nazir also has apparently announced an open defiance against the Govt, However, majority of the people do not believe because she, on one side is making open deals with Musharaf and on the other, behaving like an assailant. People are totally confused and the rumours have taken over the country. Truth is running around to find a place in society. Frustration seems to have set in and everything looks hazy and unreal. There is a constant struggle to catch hold of the truth from the rumours and deception. Pakistan First, unfortunately is becoming Pakistan Last for our ruling Junta who is not only putting but pushing themselves before the national interest. Consequently people are also losing confidence in the govt and you find nothing but decay in every walk of life. In such situation our adversaries are looking for a chance to strike at the very foundation of our country to uproot every pillar on which stands the stability and defence of the country.

Pakistan's nuclear assets are symbolic for our defence and without the nuclear weapons our country is as insecure and vulnerable from **India** as Iran is from Israel and USA. By virtue of having the nuclear weapons we feel safe and free to anchor our all efforts towards economic development, stability and prosperity.

America is fairly suspicious about our nuclear capability and has so often expressed Pakistan's nuclear weapon an Islamic bomb which is extremely dangerous for the west. They are apprehensive of its falling into the hands of extremists or Al Qaida which could be a serious threat to the entire world. They are therefore very keen to eliminate this threat at the earliest possible opportunity. Since their recent experience in Iraq and Afghanistan proved that war was no longer a lucrative business, instead of an open hostility and attack on Pakistan, they would attempt to neutralize it through betrayal of local leadership, and agents.

Mr. Bush, on many occasions has publicly expressed that he wishes to take away the nuclear capability from Pakistan. Turning deaf ears towards this is certainly closing eyes from the reality. What Americans will gain out of this is not known, but what we lose will be nothing less than a disaster.

9/11 was an incident which brought great pain and grief to Americans, at the same time, a great disaster to the Muslims as a whole and Pakistan stands as one intensely affected by it. The Muslim world was charged of this assault and Mr. Bush, immediately declared it a war of crusade without determining the facts. The attack was indeed very brutal who so ever did it, but unfortunately so was the reaction by Mr. Bush who immediately regarded it beginning of the crusade, and proved it by invading Afghanistan and Iraq without wasting any time. The mission was not intended to be confined to these two countries but was to be extended in due course to the other Muslim countries. Pakistan being the first on the list, because of its strategic importance and nuclear capability. Iraq and Afghanistan were just an excuse in this project. Iraq was destroyed to remove the hurdle in way of Israel in the region and accrue oil advantage from it. Poor Afghanistan unfortunately came in the loop of Pakistan. Basically the purpose was to secure the long desired access to the nuclear setup of Pakistan. Gen. Musharaf was found a perfect tool to reach this destination after he accepted all demands after 9/11 for a very meagre amount of money offered as a compensation for supporting USA and the allies for the invasion of Afghanistan.

Gen. Musharaf, the president and the then chief of Army staff was forced under duress to support America in Afghanistan in the so called war on terror. The Gen. surrendered on telephone and accepted all illegitimate demands to join the unholy alliance. This was indeed the first blow to Pakistan's integrity and a welcome thrust by America deep inside Pakistan to commence their long awaited aim of getting closer towards our nuclear facilities. We saw that the war on terror gradually shifted to our tribal areas inside Pakistan where the Govt of Pakistan had to deploy about seventy thousand troops to deal with the situation. At last one thousand of our troops and many thousands of civilians were killed by ourselves.

This created political turmoil and disturbance in the civil society. The pressure from political parties forced Musharaf to commit further follies like removing the Chief justice of the Supreme Court causing agitation and violence amongst civil and lawyers community. This shook the confidence of Mr. Bush in the ability of Gen. Musharaf to accomplish his ultimate motive towards nuclear pursuit. To see Gen. Musharaf's popularity diminishing, the Americans wanted to reinforce him with a political force to make him as effective as he was before this turmoil. There could be no better choice than Be-Nazir who was ever ready to join and was already struggling hard to secure her access to Pakistan. Musharaf was advised to induct her in this scenario by issuing a **National Reconciliation Ordinance** (NRO), to exempt her from all the corruption charges so that she can freely operate and reorganize the People's Party in Pakistan. She had already assured Americans for eliminating extremists and Taliban and unqualified access to Dr. Qadeer Khan. This was publicly stated by her in National and international press. The purpose was not to implicate him (as she says) in smuggling or conspiracy but probably facilitate Americans to extract all secret locations of the nuclear facilities in Pakistan as well as any deals with Iran, and other Muslim countries.

It is in the common knowledge that the nuclear setup is under Army's protection and a general perception that army is the custodian of our nuclear system and therefore is in the control of all nuclear weapons, its production, storage and operation. Army's behaviour for the last eight years reflected strictly on one point that Gen. Musharaf was the Army; because whatever he said went without any questions and challenge. He is therefore alone incharge of the command and control of the nuclear inventory also. Unfortunately he is a frightened man and a frightened person is dangerously poised to keep his wits about under acute pressure and is likely to give in when threatened of his position and status. He has displayed it before and is likely to repeat it in future under stress. It is on record that during the recent Negro-Pointe's visit to Pakistan, the Gen. very strongly brought his last ditch manoeuvre, that he could not guaranty the nuclear weapons landing at the hands of extremists if he was removed from power. I think this was an open cry to Americans whatever way one takes it.

The other custodian of our nuclear set up could be people of Pakistan or the Prime Minister of Pakistan. Keeping in view the behaviour of the Chief of Army Staff with Army, one could easily infer that the Prime Minister of Pakistan would have the same trend. Be-Nazir has been specially brought by Americans as power sharing between the Gen and herself. This is indeed the name of the game and they have very cleverly conveyed about their intention to Govt of Pakistan.

Gen Musharaf, with great reluctance has agreed to retire from Army and Gen Kiani has taken over as Army Chief. By virtue of being the commander-in-chief of the Armed Forces Mr. Musharaf is trying to keep his hold on the Army. To give a little psychological edge he has already snatched the Army house from Gen Kiani for one year to keep a close check on him. I don't know whether he would be able to keep Kiani under control and obedient to America like himself. However, it is up to Gen Kiani to accept the same status or assert his self respect as commanded by Quaid-e-Azam and Allama Iqbal.

The saner and patriotic elements of the country must realize this grave threat and its consequences in the long run. They must wake up and play their part to save the nuclear power Base of the country which has been accomplished through the poor people's blood and sacrifice of many more including some of the Muslim countries sharing with the people of Pakistan. Let us not leave it to a few generals and some self seeker civilian leaders or agents of the super power to destroy our vital assets. Let us guard them with our blood and all the strength provided by God Almighty

WATAN KI FIQER KAR NADAAN QIAMAT AANE WALI HAY

TERI BARBADIUN KE MASHWAREY HEIN AASMANU MEIN

Playing with History

2ndApril 2006

History is innocent and keeps its grace and integrity in place. It plays a very fair game by reflecting and portraying a true and exact recording of the past. It is very straight forward and respectable in its dealing and depicts a real picture of the time and happenings. If one believes in the myth of time machine he will certainly give her a credible presentation of events in a very honourable manner. History is an intrinsic reality that relates everything in an unfaltering style without any compromise or favour to one against the other. We as individuals, leaders and at times the nations, interpret it and give directions to ones own purpose and advantage, by at times construing facts to suit and maneuver the public opinion to favour ones intentions. Pakistan has been subjected to irritating criticism by US dignitaries during their recent visit to Islamabad. Let us put her case for judgment as viewed by the same history.

Mr. Bush's visit to Pakistan caused many ripples in the atmosphere when he deprived Pakistan from the same privileges and facilities as provided to India. In his opinion the history of Pakistan was responsible for this discriminatory action. Neither Mr. Bush nor our enlightened moderators clarified the negative aspects of our history that put us below the line of trust in comparison with India. However, we all felt that our ruler's silence amounted to pleading guilty. Our willingness to wait for the visit of secretary energy, Mr. Samuel Bodman for negotiating our energy requirements was indeed an acceptance of Mr. Bush's frame of mind and the undefined subject of history was put under the carpet for the sake of usual diplomatic deceptions. Mr. Samuel Bodman quickly followed Mr. Bush. His arrival was very eagerly awaited in Islamabad and lots of hopes were pinned amidst speculations of solving unresolved pleasantries left by Mr. Bush. The answer was identical and all our hopes dwindled because of the same history narrated by his president. Unlike our leaders running around the truth, our media was able to bring Mr. Bodman around the history and its main player Dr. Qadeer Khan. However, he still managed to conceal his frankness under the garb of diplomacy. Our brave leaders were still not telling us the truth openly and honestly about the essence of history meant by Mr. Bush and Mr. Bodman.

The Americans ambassador Mr. Ryan C Croker ultimately unfolded the curtains from the so called history during a debate by unmasking Dr.Qadeer's status as part of this history and had the guts to pronounce that no Qadeer will be born in Pakistan in future. I wish he could also say about Mr. Bush in the same sense.

This was one side of the history that created so much discrimination by treating Pakistan as apple of another tree from that of India, by all the dignitaries of the United States. However, besides Dr. Qadeer there are other perspectives of our history with America. I would like to narrate that aspect of history without any recrimination but certainly with a reminder and retrospect that friend is a friend, no matter how strong and big he is. I do understand the interest of countries and nations but there are some principles to be reckoned with. Israel is not even one fifth of Pakistan but this kind of disparity is not applied to her by our Big friend. In fact to safeguard its security and facilitate its war potential all kinds of help and assistance is provided to ensure her control on big Arab neighbors; not to speak of their inhumane and barbaric treatment of Palestinians.

Our history does not start and end with Dr. Qadeer. It started in 1950 friendship treaty against communism when no other country in this region was ready to stand by United States. India was then playing in the lap of Soviets when we provided a vital communication facility to monitor the communists and Soviet activities from bases in Pakistan. It was from Peshawar (Pakistan) from where the spy flights of U-2 aircraft used to takeoff on spying mission to USSR. When young Powel was shot down and caught over Russia, Mr. Nikita Khrushchev Chairman of the then Soviet Union marked 'Peshawar' on his map and threatened to destroy Pakistan for this act of aggressive collaboration with our friend USA. This happens to be also part of our history too.

We also remember the debacle of 1971 when India attacked Pakistan with all the backing of their friend USSR. We kept waiting for the arrival of 7th fleet which never reached the Indian Ocean till we lost

East Pakistan. It appeared as if it was all made up to cut Pakistan to her size by our friends and enemies alike. The unforgettable humiliations suffered by us are still very fresh in our minds as part of the same history. Mind you we were official ally of USA in SEATO and CENTO alliance.

The history does not mark time at one place; it keeps moving and watching fools like us. We again fell in the trap of our friends and became front line fighter in 1979 when Soviets invaded Afghanistan. This time the stakes were very high. They wanted revenge from Soviets for their part in Vietnam and Korea and we became their tool for the purpose. Irrespective of why and how it happened, but please don't take away our credit of defeating the Soviets and giving them the gifts of becoming the sole superpower of the world.

Then came 9/11 and your war against terrorism. We were enticed, threatened or whatever, we again became your front line fighter and ally against Afghanistan, our neighbour and all time friend, brother in Islam and above all our vital battle depth. We stood by **US** and destroyed our depth, demolished Taliban brothers and accepted our enemies, the Northern alliance to power under duress. We still supported **you** everywhere against fight with terrorism.

We killed our own citizens in North and South Waziristan to trace out **US** enemies; not ours. We still have eighty thousand troops deployed in that area to cover **your** back in Afghanistan. What more sacrifice is expected from us, to change our history to your liking, which will entitle us to have the same privilege and facilities as our enemy, India.

We object to your imbalanced treatment vis-à-vis India just because of Dr. Qadeer. India's this kind of history started in 1974 when everyone including Dr. Henry kasinger turned a deaf ear on our cries. From where did India get this technology? I am sure they were not born with this. Let us therefore not talk of Dr. Qadeer only; many big traders in Europe and America are involved in the history of proliferation. We love Dr. Qadeer for his services to Pakistan. No Musharaf can take that away even if **Mr. Bush** is at his back.

Our history is indeed better than India **who** has always been playing against US interest except for their own trade and economic benefits. What more sacrifices **you** would expect from us to rewrite our history. We have even retreated from our stand on Kashmir, just to facilitate your friendship with India. In the end we leave it to American people to judge the fair play of their leaders for administering the worldly affairs as "Sole Super Power" in the world.

An Open Letter to General (R) Parvez Musharaf

Please Return to Your BRADARI

23rd June 2008

I am not a registered member of the ex-servicemen society but I consider myself as part of this BRADRI with whom I spent 25 years of my useful life and learnt so much of physical and brain work that in my retirement now I cherish the memories of those achievements during my service.

I did my intermediate and joined Pakistan Airforce as a young man of 18 years. Rest all education, management skills, administrative, and organizational abilities in life is a gift of my service to me. I feel grateful to my ex-commanders and seniors from whom I learnt to live not only in my service but found to manage my affairs very well in my civil life after retirement. My association with ex-servicemen is, therefore inherent and natural and I am indeed proud of it.

During my service I was assigned to modernize Pakistan Air Defence System. With my team we fabricated a system which was the best at that time and is second to none in the world even today. In the three wars with India the PAF Air Defence System played a vital role to save the country. I am only relating the above to stress that all my professional capabilities were groomed only by the Air Force and through the Air Force only.

At the beginning of the present turmoil in the country I have written the following few papers to remind you to honour your own commitments of "Pakistan First" and handover the country to the legitimate incumbents to govern. Some of them may not have been published for plain writing not suiting our English born news editors and may be lying in their databanks.

1. Enough is enough—Wrap up the end sensibly (24th May 2007)
2. A deal disgraceful for all (30th August 2007)

3. God knows Mullah Omar—Who is Karzai (26 August 2007)
4. Mekhial Gorbachev in Pakistan (04 November 2007)
5. An unbecoming address (24 November 2007)
6. Guard your Nuclear Assets (12 December 2007)

Please forgive me writing directly to you but I consider you as involuntary member of Ex-Servicemen BRADARI.

Mr. President; Like all other Generals, Air Marshals, and Admirals, you are also one of the stems out of the same root. You have achieved your manhood from the same academy as all other generals and senior officers who were members of Armed Forces. I am sure you realize that you are not a product from some super university with a special PhD degree to claim your genius better than those who commanded the same establishment before you. Some of them were more effective than you in the crisis and war like situation. The history speaks for itself and reflects its own assessment and impression in accordance with the performance shown by the individual in each event. People are the best judges to shape the conclusion. Those who believe the people's verdict are propitious and those who are victim of egoism face delusion at the end. To counsel with your old colleagues in crisis is like perceiving diagnosis from a group of competent doctors during life saving moments.

Mr. President, your senior colleagues are some of those distinguished commanders who have excelled in all walks of their professional careers during their active service of the country. I am sure your interaction with them would improve your good governance and prevision of certain essentials facing the country today.

Air Marshal (R) Mohammad Asghar Khan commanded the PAF for 8 years and prepared it to meet the challenge of three times bigger Indian Airforce in war. This was proved in Ran-of-Kutch, 1965 and 1971 wars. After retirement his political career was a symbol of truth and adherence to noble principals. Even Mr. Buhtto could not entice him away from this path in spite of very lucrative offers to join him befool this poor illiterate nation. He simply refused to fall prey to his stratagem. Although it looked as a downfall at that time but this was indeed his victory and not failure in real politics.

Air Marshal Noor Khan succeeded him to carry out this mission skillfully and in an outstanding manner. During his active service he was assigned to establish PIA and I can proudly say that he was able to place a sick airline at one of the fifth best airlines of the world. After him unfortunately PIA could not maintain that position and reputation till today. As Incharge of the sports, he succeeded in bringing Pakistan hockey, squash, and cricket on world's top ranking teams. He also suggested a few fundamental changes in the world sport's which earned him a name by the world sports bodies for all times to come.

General Aslam Baig Mirza deserves praise for voluntarily giving up the power bestowed on him through an act of nature and invited the chairman senate to take over their long awaited responsibilities as a democratic president of the country. He certainly was the first general in Pakistan, help democracy get on the track and maintain its course. He strictly followed the constitution and retired at the end of his tenure as the Army Chief. We as a nation must give him his due credit earned honestly and willfully.

Generals, Hammed Gul, Moinuddin Haider, Durani, and others who you call as pseudo intellectuals tried their best to remind you, in their own way to adopt the constitutional manner to end the crisis.

Mr. President, you may be gifted with a streak of a genius in your veins to steer this country to a glorious path but you have to convince this nation about your personal credibility. Unfortunately you failed in Kargil, you surrendered to a secretary of United Sates on a telephone call; Even **Colonel Gaddafi** took three years to surrender. You gave-up our principal stand on Kashmir. In spite of having absolute power for 10 years you could not bring any real economic progress and prosperity. I am not narrating quite a number of other follies like referendum, your personal election, and declaration of emergency as Chief of the Army Staff which are haunting this nation today. Please be advised that you are an actor and we are the spectators, we have the privilege and prerogative to appreciate your performance at the stage. You may not follow **Mr. Zardari** who thinks his big smile and irrelevant talks are very impressive and appreciative by the people of Pakistan.

Your retired comrade at arms having graduated from the same institute as yourself, having much more experience in practical life, offered sincere advice through letters to sit together and discuss a way out to save this country from the crisis created by you intentionally or unintentional. They should have been accommodated as a blessing in disguise by you rather than rejecting it as an incompetent advice. May I have the liberty to suggest that you are one of us, belonging to the same roots, learning from the same university, and having brought-up through the same social setup, to return to your family and invite some of these retired colleagues and through mutual consultations and deliberations seek a way out to bring the country back on a path of honour, dignity, and glory even if it amounts to a temporary setback. By refusing to interact with your own colleagues, you were forced to accept people like **Salman Taseer** who had the audacity to abuse your own generals in front of you. In fact in etiquette of rural society he was directly addressing you with all his BAZARI language.

I am sure you may be aware that recently **Mr. Barak Obama**, the US Presidential Candidate during his recent victory speech decided to invite at least 40 ex-generals to discuss the security plans in Afghanistan and Iraq to save his country from an ultimate insult.

You may be imagining an escape or extension due to Iranian/US escalation in the near future but we can see no formidable change expected for your survival as President. How about taking a bold decision to face the unknown bravely. Baradari, I am sure would do everything to condone your failing judiciously.

In the end I request you to "LAUT AAWO MERAY PARDESI BAHAAR AAEI HAY."

"Oh my lost bird come back to your flock and enjoy."

The Leadership Crisis and its' Consequence in Pakistan

20ᵗʰ July 2008

It is surprising to note that 160 million people are helpless to produce a single leader who could take her out of the crisis in which a pigmy dictator, who could not see a few yards away has brought this nation to this state of affairs. The 2008 election unfortunately picked-up another unelected self styled and self seeker mini dictator Mr. Zardari who is driving the biggest political party and its leaders like a flock of sheep. The second big party is also like a hostage in the hands of Mr. Zardari. Mr. Nawaz Sharif seems to be as helpless as 160 million people of this country. He was one leader who could at least had the courage to say 'NO' to big powers when he thought it was against the interest of the nation.

General (R) Musharaf has been ruling this country for the last 8 years but unfortunately on the whims and direction of the only superpower, to stay in power. National interest was attached to American interest, irrespective of its relevancy to Pakistan. It appears that General Musharaf and Zardari are driving the same car with a common destination and even the people party's leaders cannot deviate them from this course. If they all have decided to sell Pakistan for a few bucks to insure that they stay in power, and the nation is not ready to exercise her willpower to remove them, the result will be alarming and might end up in precarious situation because "As you sow so shall you reap".

20ᵗʰ Century witnessed a two superpower drama in which both America and Soviet Union were at each others' throat in every conflict to drive benefit from one over the other. The whole world was divided in two groups, the Soviets and the American block. Each Superpower was carefully handling their friends and allies in favor or against in accordance with their own interest. The Third World's weak and poor nations felt safer because of this divide and rivalry. In this context both the powers were trying to bring each other down through conflicts and acquisition of economic benefits. In this very rivalry America was engaged and defeated in Vietnam and Korea through Soviet hooking with tremendous economic loss and indignity to USA.

America was looking for an opportunity to avenge this insult. This was provided by Soviets through the invasion of Afghanistan in 1979.

Pakistan is a country whom nature has provided a remarkable strategic importance that no big powers can afford to ignore her. Whenever in the past there was a conflict of interest by the Superpowers in this region they could not afford to overlook Pakistan's involvement in their favor. During the Soviet invasion of Afghanistan it was basically the Americans who actually appealed the whole Muslim world to apply the option of Jihad, if there was any left, to fight and defeat this polar bear and save this brother Muslim country from a Godless society.

Pakistan was lured into this challenge to organize the Jihad force to face this giant. It became the headquarters of Mujahedeen from all over the Muslim world to be disciplined, trained, and organized in the modern warfare tactics. The entire logistic support and weapons were of course provided by the USA to fight the Soviets.

Pakistan stood like a rock to fight and ultimately defeat the USSR who retreated with extra ordinary casualties, total economic collapse and eventually was broken as a Superpower. Since then there is only one Superpower in the world, the "United States of America". That was the contribution and gift of Pakistan toward its' ally, **America**.

Now it was the American turn to repay Pakistan for its loyalties and efforts for the glory of USA. They ensured that Pakistan does not grow out of proportion and achieve an important place in the Muslim world. The first action was:

1. To impose Pressler Ammendments.
2. To impound all American war equipment inspite of the payments made.
3. To impose restrictions on other countries to sell anything that had some American Machinery element in it.

61

4. Decrease Economic Aid to Pakistan to cripple her economically and militarily.
5. To ensure that Pakistan remains under Indian hegemony in future.
6. To force Pakistan to withdraw support from freedom fighters, fighting for the cause of Kashmir.

The burden of 5 million refugees almost crippled Pakistan economically, along with the overflow of war and klashonkof culture deteriorating her security and law and order situation. Pakistan became the most insecure and economically weak country in this region as a result of Afghan war. We unfortunately did not have a strong national leader to reap the reward of the sacrifices made in the Afghan war but instead accepted obediently the above restrictions. The war lords and other freedom fighter groups created catastrophe in Afghanistan which affected Pakistan's internal security in a big way.

The stability in Afghanistan was finally secured after establishment of Taliban government which brought some kind of semblance of peace in Afghanistan.

Then came the devil of 9/11, that made the Americans immediately vomit all the anti-Muslim hidden agenda to demonstrate as a sole superpower to establish their authority and see that no one in the world could challenge it. No Russia or China could raise any voice of interference in American designs. Most of the dirt fell on Muslims because they were accused of threatening their authority through 9/11. No one knows who was responsible but never the less Muslims became the target as most of the Hijackers were fixed to be Muslims.

First on the agenda was Afghanistan, because of Osama bin Laden and the Mujahideen. Iraq, the second because of oil and its' military strength to challenge Israel. Pakistan, the third because of her Nuclear weapons and assets. Iran the next because of independent policies and future Nuclear threat to Israel. The plan though seems to be carrying on in order, however "man proposes and God disposes" is working like always and **Mr. Bush** seems to be struck at the first rendezvous.

Afghanistan the poorest country in the world and already destroyed and demolished during 10 years old war with Russia was attacked by USA with an excuse of protecting Osama Bin Laden, allegedly involved in 9/11 attack. Daisy cutter, cluster and oxygen bombs were dropped like rain to kill the poorest people of the poorest country to occupy it. It was also a warning to other poor and weak nations that this treatment could be extended to them and there was no one in the world to challenge.

They called this a war against terror and General Parvez Musharaf, the dictator president of Pakistan was threatened to join this coalition and provide all support facilities like logistic and provision of air bases to American Forces fighting for occupation of Afghanistan; failing which Pakistan would be brought to stone ages. This, **war like gimmick** was accepted by the COWARD COMMANDO as real; who surrendered on a telephone call for mere $3 billion compensation. Pakistan was thus made to join the category of mercenary in a so called war on terror against their own brothers in faith and neighbor.

Who initiated war in Afghanistan? Undoubtedly it was America who forced this war on Taleban government and occupied this country and is continuing this occupation by force. Is it not the right of these people to fight and drive these invaders out of their country like they did in case of the Soviets? I think the Pakistan government must turn their coats like Americans did to Pakistan at the end of Afghan war. The Mujahedeen from all over the world must also fulfill the commitments as performed in case of Russian invasion. I think the day is not far when the present situation is reversed in due course, in favor of divine justice.

The war has now extended to the frontiers of Pakistan and NATO forces are accusing that most of Taliban forces are regrouping in the tribal areas of Pakistan to organize attacks in Afghanistan. Osama Bin Ladin is also hiding in this very area. They also seem to have the approval of the Pakistan government to attack inside Pakistan on the basis of American and NATO intelligence.

This authority may ultimately be extended in search of our nuclear assets and neutralize it as a legitimate action in accordance with their original plan.

Fighting in FATA and Swat is like a cancer creeping inch by inch to the heart of our country.

Most of our own people being killed by our own army and suicide bombers. Who is planning this? It reminds me of Iraq where I served on deputation in 1968-1971. During these years I never heard of any Shia Sunni differences or fight. The position now is completely different. Iraqis are now killing each other in hundreds every day. That very disease is being induced in Pakistan by those who had produced these germs in Iraq. I bet Americans know it and they must be confronted with it and should be requested to solve this problem.

To stop the onslaught you got to face it with courage and conviction. Safeguard your interest and **convert your submission** into mutual interest and benefit. This will be more lasting in the long run. Americans must be told to be friends not masters. They were told this 42 years before that undue dictation brings hatred inspite of big favors.

A real leader with courage and conviction can change the scenario on equal terms and standings. If we had a leader of wisdom and resolute we could have forced Kashmir issue in 1979 before jumping into Afghan war or negotiating a reasonable surrender after 9/11.

How could Musharaf look into the eyes of Americans with his personal illegitimate status?

How can Zardari face Americans with a NRO background and his Mr. 10 percent repute?

I hope this Leadership famine ends through nature's blessings and someone like Imran Khan or Nawaz Sharif appears at the helm of affairs. I have faith in God Almighty Allah that the strategic situation of Pakistan itself is a guarantee of her survival and respectable place in the community of nations.

9/11 IS COMING AGAIN

27ᵗʰ July 2008

So says George W Bush Jr while addressing some official gathering a few days ago. How he knows need a good guess by anyone to determine the time and place. When the first occurred, he was addressing children in classroom at Sarasota, Florida, on the morning of 9/11. When he was told, it at once revealed on him that it was Muslim crusade against America. He later felt embarrassed of his prompt disclosure and he had to appear before prominent Muslims in a mosque to shed off his humiliations. However, he did what he wanted to do. The Muslims were targeted to demonstrate his vision of protective philosophy for America. Osama bin Laden, a tiny figure representing Al Qaida was made to appear a great genius who could manoeuvre a mission impossible over America while sitting in the mountains and caves of Afghanistan, being totally illiterate in the art of air warfare like his hosts, the Taliban. The whole incident was so deciphered to the simple people of America that they immediately accepted a retaliatory attack on the world's poorest country by their commander in chief. What happened after is known to the entire world and what is happening today is another plan emerging like making a mountain out of a mole hill. Iraq was another victim whose blood is still oozing out of the wounds inflicted by a super power along with her poodle, as depicted by the British press of their then Prime Minister Mr. Tony Blair.

However, that was the first 9/11 that shook the entire world after the Second World War. The World War, of course was outcome of Hitler's evil ambitions and over confidence to conquer Europe and maybe the world to become a 'super power'. Similarly, whether the west believes it or not, the first 9/11 was the outcome of Israel's behaviour and atrocities committed against Palestinians and Arabs, with the unconditional singular support the Americans provided to Israel to continue the cruelties towards the real land owners. If at all it was from Arabs it was a natural reaction of the aggrieved for the inhuman and savage treatment to them. Whether it was done by Arabs or the Jew's planning of the futuristic exploitations, the cause was Palestine and the American undue and unjust support to Israel.

65

The second 9/11 may well have the same origin but could surface under different arrangement. The war in Afghanistan and subsequently to Iraq has involved almost half of the world which includes all the NATO countries, Japan and Australia. Al Qaida, a small group restricted to Afghanistan has now spread out to many other countries through the courtesy of Mr. Bush and party.

The outright and unreasonable support to Israel has practically transformed America as a 'new Israel'. A small localised affair of Middle East has now expanded to the entire Muslim world and the obvious target seems to be, the 'new Israel'. Mr. Bush Jr may well be right in expecting another 9/11 very soon.

The Arabs sitting on the oil reservoir, vital for the world to exist, have been painfully watching the unreasonable attitude of America and the west in favour of Israel for a long time now. The people of the Arab world are gunning for their rulers for the cowardly character and compromising approach towards a principle stand against Israel. When Mahmoud Ahmadinejad says he would like to put a last nail in the coffin of Israel, he does not only mean to do it by himself. He also takes into account the people of the entire Arab World who are concerned with it more than the Iranians. It is up to America and the west to keep a check on their protégée otherwise the charge is being framed against both, the old and the new Israel. The time is the biggest judge and shall bring justice. It maybe late but it must come.

The war on terror is taking a big toll on human lives in tribal areas of Pakistan. Similar situation is faced by Taliban in Afghanistan and areas bordering with Pakistan. People, both in Pakistan and Afghanistan are fed up and resent this war. The governments on both sides are facing this menace under duress from America. It is a matter of time how long these governments would be able to resist the pressure from their people.

Destruction of Afghanistan perceivably is not the aim of European NATO countries. They would like to see economically prosperous Afghanistan rather than leaving it in ruins. Similarly the people of England are flabbergasted on the behaviour of their government in creating an unnecessary war zone and getting their troops killed at the same time buying ill will of Afghans. American case is different; they take pleasure in creating adventures and ultimately leave when it becomes unbearable to stay.

Palestinians are not very appreciative of big leader's visits and donations to boost their economy but they resent the lopsided behaviour of the west, specially the Americans and the British in favour of Israel. Mr. Gordon Brown's recent visit to Palestine and prescription of thirty million pounds were though a welcome relief for the poor but such beggar like gestures are indeed very hypocritical and painful when you turn a deaf ear to the basic rights of the Palestinians on their own land. This creates more resentment and frustration in human relationship rather than bringing long term goodwill.

I am indeed very sorry about the five British soldiers kidnapped for the last one year, where one of them committed suicide in captivity. How about being fair for once and admit that the whole of Iraq has been hi-jacked by America and Britain for the last six years? Every rational citizen of UK must raise their eye brows and shout against their government for the excesses committed against Iraqis for no reason. I am sure if there was any analytical study of a dead human brain, the one belonging to this deceased would have cried out to leave Iraq.

Barack Obama and John McCain's contradictory statements on Iraq has put Iraqis in a strange feeling of hope and despair where one wants to withdraw and the other wants to continue indefinitely from Iraq. This indirectly conveys a considerable mistrust in the current American policy. The impatient African blood and an experienced racist trend hopefully compromise on the issues of foreign occupation by American troops.

The recent foreign visit by Barack Obama of Germany and UK has indeed shown an emergence of new style leader. His speech of tearing the walls between Christians, Muslims, and Jews are indeed a very welcome sermon, if it is not only restricted to only one side of the hemisphere. However, tearing the wall is meaning full only if you can stand in open and embrace each other as equals, otherwise it would be better to keep the walls and live safely in each other's environments like a good and trusted neighbours.

It is not enough for a guardian super power to speak of justice; it has to be done and also seen. Once everybody feels its application for poor and rich, weak and strong nations alike, and equal treatment for all, there will be no 9/11 again, failing which I would agree with Mr. Bush, another 9/11 maybe coming soon.

GOING BACK TO STONE AGE

9ᵗʰAugust 2008

The drama of 'back to stone age' was played soon after 9/11 when Gen. Musharaf, the President of Pakistan surrendered on a telephone call from the secretary of State Colin Powell and he accepted to become part of the war on terror against Afghanistan. Afghanistan was subjected to carpet bombing with all the modern bombs available in the inventory of USA and is still being dealt with in the same fashion when ever required. I have since never been in Afghanistan to see the picture of stone age after these bombing, however, the people in Afghanistan are still fighting very bravely with the occupying forces inspite of the inclusion of NATO forces from all over Europe. The latest evidence available reveals that NATO forces are under constant fear of defeat because of the tough resistance of the people (including Taliban), and most of the NATO countries are looking for an escape route to quit.

After almost seven years we in Pakistan are still under a big scare and some of our leaders and intellectuals like Gen. Musharaf, Sheikh Rasheed, Mushahid Hussein, and S.M Zafar are still frightening the nation with American threat of taking Pakistan back to the Stone Age. I am sure living in the Stone Age must be horrendous but certainly living in comfort and luxury at the cost of freedom and respect is equally dreadful. The drama has though grown fairly old but it seems the fear of it still prevails in the heart of our timid leadership and the dictator who initially got the show on the road in the first place. They are still trying to support war on terror by fighting with our own people in the tribal areas in the aid of our so called friends. This is an unending war with the Afghan's brave sons of the soil and our own brothers in faith.

I have a very hazy picture about the Stone Age through film documentaries and I hope our leaders are not taking literal meaning of those pictures about the threat depicted by the Americans. However, the common people in the streets feel that no matter with how much density the Americans bomb us, we will still be left with a match to light and enough bread to fill our tummies. Water and air of course are God's gift to survive and nobody can take that away. Surely we could keep our heads high for not accepting a defeat without fighting. In a war there is no such thing as defeat; it is victory or death, no matter which way you look at it. We have had a taste of defeat in 1971 which unfortunately happened basically through our own people in East Pakistan. We are still licking those wounds with an urge to revenge from India one day.

The story of getting Pakistan to Stone Age is not a new one. It started with Mr. Nikita Khrushchev, president of Soviet Union, when he declared that he had marked Peshawar on his Map in 1962 when an American spy plan U-2 had taken off from Peshawar for reconnaissance of Russian instillations. It was shot down by Russians and the captured pilot, Garry Powel had confessed to have taken off from Peshawar. The Russians took nine years to fulfil their desire when they helped India to break up Pakistan. For an average Pakistani it was no less distressing than landing in a Stone Age. Those were the days when we sacrificed half of Pakistan and our friends could not reach to save us from the enemies, made because of them. The same friends are off to take us to Stone Age, and none of our leaders have the courage to stand up to this threat and remind them about our past sacrifices.

Then came 1965 war with India. How we landed in that situation is still not very clear, but we came out well at all fronts. The whole world recognized our supremacy over India in this war. The Muslim world acknowledged our victory and almost all, even those who were apparently against us, sought our assistance in the military field.

Pakistan government was approached by all prominent Muslim countries to reorganize their Armed forces. Saudi Arab, Jordan, and UAE, requested to completely overhaul their systems and update their Air Forces, which intrigued most of the European countries and America for the purchase of their equipment. Syria, Iraq, and Egypt also requested to send contingents from Air force and Army to review their inadequacies. It indeed reflected a strong dependence and influence by these countries on Pakistan, which was basically not acceptable to the West. They were indirectly suspicious of a hidden future threat to Israel. Since then Pakistan was being chased to be cut in size and strength lest it becomes a permanent force in the region. 1971 war with

India gave them an opportunity of a century to break up Pakistan and set aside their misgivings once and for all.

However, Pakistan recovered under the leadership of Mr. Zulfiqar Ali Bhutto and soon after became the seventh Nuclear State of the World. This resulted in a greater irritant than before for the West and especially to our friend America. Since then Pakistan was targeted with all sorts of embargoes and prejudices like Pressler's amendments, economic restrictions, military equipment prohibition, etc.

They were also after our nuclear assets and looking for a chance to neutralize it as soon as possible and at any cost. A little respite came through because of 9/11. However, 9/11 brought new dimension to the world situation. Who so ever planned it, had a real devil's mind with the ability to correctly predict the effect of this on the people he had actually programmed. No one up till now has conducted a serious enquiry to find out the truth. Every stake holder is drawing his own conclusion and colour it to suit his own objective. Countries like Iraq, Afghanistan, and Pakistan, are the victim of that planning. There is likely a chance of its expanding to Iran and Syria; God only knows when it will come to an end.

Affluent people in Pakistan are getting into a strange type of psychological depression that without the help of west they will be losing all the necessities of life including education and technology. They therefore need to give in something to secure the above prerequisites of life. I was sitting with a few retired Army generals, on their life time vacation in London, the other day. They were so obsessed with the western technology and power that they literally seemed suffering from acute inferiority complex and defeat from inside. I tried my best to convince them that the western technology is a reality, but nobody can put a lid on technology, discoveries or innovations. Sooner or later it will come at your own doorstep if "seek and ye shall find" is your motto. After all we have become a nuclear state on our own. By the way many renowned western universities are advertising in Pakistan to buy students and earn money. We have no reason to be scared of anything or feel inferior from.

Look at the Chinese, the western world wouldn't talk to them in 1950's and flirt only with Taiwan. Chairman Mao Tse-Tung and subsequently Chiang Kai-Shek, pulled the whole world towards them with the strength of conviction and their principles. The Americans pleaded them to join their world even at the cost of their protégée, Taiwan. We cannot compare ourselves with China, but certainly we are no less than Malaysia.

The Arabs on the other hand preferred to lead an easy and comfortable life and enjoy by selling off their oil. They have stopped struggling like their forefathers who had marched on Spain, France, and Poland, on their horse's back. But now they are not capable to ward off a handful of Jews from their own soil.

The days of Stone Age is part of the history only and no one can take you back to that stage. Every physical force is met with a force of conviction which may demand more sacrifice but ensures victory at the end. Those who dare, empty threats have no significance for them. They stand on their feet in peace and war. The only common platform is the mutual respect and regard for each other.

Farwell Bouquet for General Pervez Musharaf

16th August 2008

Pervez Musharaf would certainly deserve a red rose's bouquet on his departure (if he departs) after ruling Pakistan for almost nine years with absolute authority and power without any opposition from within or outside the country. He had the audacity to get the sitting PM arrested and put in jail for almost three years and later forced him in exile to Saudi Arabia for ten years. He got himself convinced that Mr. Nawaz Sharif would be a spent force in these many years or gone out of circulation. It never occurred once in his mind that "Man proposes and God disposes".

With his case now pending in the National Assembly for impeachment, many agencies are passing different opinion on his expected exit. Some want his trial, some are satisfied with impeachment result and forgive and forget policy. A few want him to resign and request for a safe exit, yet there are a few ready to grant him a graceful exit and leave the country. General Pervez is a person of unique standing in the world today. For his following incomparable services, he certainly deserves something unique from the nation.

i.) He staged a coup d'état in 1999 and removed a democratically elected government with 2/3 majority in the National Assembly. He was the first man to obtain three years rule from his appointed judiciary with the specific authority to make changes in the constitution.

ii.) He designated his own PM, an American agent and got him elected from his own created National Assemble.

iii.) He was the first President to break his own promise to remove his uniform in 2004 in accordance with the agreement with MMA on the 7th amendment in constitution and a solemn pledge to the nation on television.

iv.) He has a unique achievement to fight for Presidential election in uniform from the outgoing assemblies and win with great majority.

v.) He has an unmatched performance of declaring martial law twice in his tenure

vi.) He was the first man in uniform to dismiss the Chief Justice of Pakistan and sixty judges and putting Chief Justice, his family, and a few judges under house arrest.

vii.) He was the one and only one to surrender on a telephone call from the American Secretary of State after 9/11.

viii.) He was the only one to declare killing his own people in Baluchistan and Tribal Area.

ix.) He was the first one to sell his people to CIA for money.

x.) He was the first President of Pakistan to offer India with so many options on Kashmir that our claim on Kashmir got lost somewhere in the swamp of those obscure and puzzling options.

Every traditional Army in the world has a general practice that the serving Generals have the privilege to consult the retired colleagues during national crisis. General Musharaf refused to even talk to his own colleagues, his instructors, and very capable learned seniors whom he called useless and pseudo intellectuals. There is, though no rule as such to seek advice from old Generals but it has been happening in Pakistan and all over the world. **However, I wouldn't suggest General Kyani, the present Chief of Army staff to consult General Musharaf in the present crisis**.

The retired Generals on their own had been requesting him to call it a day and hand over the power to the democratically elected people and revive the judiciary removed by him erroneously. But he dismissed their counsel and suggestions as worthless. Besides, most of the world wide survey reports, at least 80% of our own intelligential wanted Musharaf to resign and vacate the presidency. Even his American friends wanted some kind of reconciliation to provide him a safe and honourable exit.

I was reading the column of Mr. Irshad Ahmed Haqqani in The Daily Jung the other day, where he had suggested that if Musharaf is willing to resign he should be given a safe passage and excused of all crimes related to his takeover from the legitimate government in 1999. His subsequent crimes of violating the constitution may also be set aside in lieu of this resignation and providing respite to this poor nation. I am fan of Mr. Haqqani and have all the regard for his candid and very honest analysis of national problems. However, I would like to make him a judge and request for a judgement on a man who has bulldozed this young country for eight years as if it was his personal property. Is the law in Pakistan made only to punish the poor and hungry people for small offenses for saving their children and themselves from hunger and disease? What about those big fish who swallow the national wealth like a piece of meal? They must be at least brought on board to show their black faces to the nation. Their use of power and authority to damage the integrity and honour of the nation must be brought to people's court and I would request Mr. Haqqani also to pass the judgment fairly and judiciously.

In situation like this an honest self critique is the only medicine to cure oneself, provided it is based on the truth and not on one's crony's customary sermons.

Unfortunately when trouble comes, it comes in brigades. When small things fail to cause any sensation, they tend to grow bigger and slowly turn into mountains which become difficult to cross. One has to, then find a bypass to overcome these problems otherwise a brigade would look much bigger than its actual volume, and indeed becomes difficult to surpass. This is what happened to our friend Musharaf. He didn't take any notice, or shall we say didn't care about small things. He seemed drunk with power and authority and couldn't notice the storm developing out of mild winds under his own feet. Even now there is a chance to save the situation if he can quietly accept a farewell bouquet and disappear in the crowd.

Zardari the President

26ᵗʰ August 2008

When Benazir's marriage was arranged with Zardari in 1987, it was generally understood to have been set forth to exhibit an Islamic obligation and obedience applicable to all young Muslims. To my information it was basically manoeuvred to protect her from any salacious rumours that might affect her future political career. Zardari was made merely a casual husband. In fact the subsequent rumours about their relationship almost confirmed to be on the same pattern.

However Zardari unexpectedly started behaving like a real husband and exercised full authority, inspite of her being a Prime Minister and acted to show his character as traditionally expected by a husband in our society. Having the privilege to be PM's husband he started interfering in administration and other government functionaries so much that the people party leaders, workers and people in general openly criticized Benazir's government as completely helpless to stop his involvement in state affairs, especially in purchase of foreign equipment. He was involved in almost all big deals with the intension of receiving commissions through the local agents and at times through the principals of foreign companies. The deals became so apparent and visible that he became to be known as Mr. 10% by the large number of people of Pakistan. He became so strong that Benazir as PM could not stop him interfering even in her own family affairs and relationship with her real brother Murtaza Bhutto, who was ultimately killed in Karachi and unfortunately Zardari was one of the accused in that case. Mr. Mumtaz Bhutto even now feels that Zardari was the main culprit and Benazir had no courage to ask him to appear before the judicial enquiry.

Ultimately it became so obvious and conspicuous that the President of Pakistan primarily from the People's Party, Mr. Farooq Leghari had to dismiss Benazir's government to get rid of all these irregularities in administration and government affairs. Mr. Zardari was apprehended for numerous corruption charges and put in jail. Benazir was equally made responsible for the corruption in which Mr. Zardari was involved.

Majority of the people, at that time actually believed that it was on the behest of Benazir that Zardari was manoeuvring all these deals. Some hard core Jialas thought that Benazir was innocent, only Zardari was to blame for everything. This philosophy was utterly unacceptable because without BB, Zardari was a non-entity. All the money so earned was going in their joint account or purchase of property abroad. The cases had even been registered by some foreign governments against them for drug trafficking and money laundering from Pakistan.

An average man with ordinary intelligence will understand that Zardari couldn't do it without Benazir's explicit consent and direction. She had the control of things in the government; Zardari couldn't have moved an inch without her. Indeed they both were undoubtedly the conniving partners.

Benazir left Pakistan in the year 2000 and remained in self exile for almost eight years in Dubai. During these years she kept in touch with Pakistan politics with the hope to return in good days. In the mean time Mr. Zardari remained in jail under trial for his corruption crimes within and out of Pakistan. After his bail petition he was allowed to leave Pakistan to see his wife and children. He never returned to Pakistan since then except when General Musharaf forgave both of them, and because of them hundreds of other criminals through NRO. This was done because of American desire to support General Musharaf's dwindling popularity in Pakistan.

Benazir returned to Pakistan in Oct '07. She was unfortunately chased by hidden forces to follow their instruction in the newly emerging political situation. She was very enlightened leader with her hands on the pulse of general public. After watching the political climate she immediately realized that she couldn't openly follow the given course because it would deprive her from the people's support in coming elections. It was very sad and unfortunate that her changing course brought her tragic death in Rawalpindi on 27th Dec'07. We all mourn her death because we saw a new Benazir emerging out of a new political arena in Pakistan. However, most of us are quite skeptical about the legacy she unfortunately left as a parting gift to Pakistan. The poor hungry orphans of PPP leadership welcomed Zardari with open hands and mouth to continue the same old political business in Pakistan. Unfortunately most of them have got used to greeting such a leader and creating opportunity to fill their empty pockets. Zardari at once grabbed this opportunity to take over the leadership to drive these orphans of PPP to a stage that they have all agreed to nominate him as the President of Pakistan.

After going through the Zardari Benazir era of 1993-96 and the news reports of that time from media and their speculations, I was quite convinced that it was all done with BB Zardari mutual consent. I bet every sensible PPP leader, including my friend Aitezaz Ahsan firmly believe from their inner heart that it was true, but they purposely turned a deaf ear to their conscience and still accepted Zardari as their leader for some reasons well known to them. They need to put their hands on their children's head and swear that Zardari and Benazir were not involved in corruption as partners. Mian Nawaz Sharif, Maulana Fazal ul Rehman, and Asfand Yaar Wali are also aware of Zardari's deeds yet they are all ready to bargain and support Zardari as the president of Pakistan.

Mr. Zardari might have been an innocent looking gentleman to Benazir and her mother before marriage but now he is a well known character in Pakistan and his smile is not as innocent as many would imagine it to be. We have got rid of Gen. Musharaf with great difficulty and I hope we don't get 'out of the frying pan into the fire'.

A short synopsis of Political Parties of Pakistan

27ᵗʰ Nov. 2008

Political parties were my favourite subject even when I was serving in the Pakistan Air force. Firstly because I was a voter and every voter has a responsibility to vote for a suitable, honest and reasonable candidate. Secondly to vote for a right minded genuine party with a sympathetic manifesto for the people and progressive program for the country. As a voter my main emphasis was a good candidate. A political party which did not nominate a good candidate did not deserve to secure that particular seat for which an unbecoming candidate was projected.

Out of all the parties in circulation **Pakistan People Party** (PPP) was the one which fascinated me the most because of its program and manifesto. It coincided with my own views. I being a village product had an urge to do something for my people to improve their standard of living, education and health. This all was provided in the manifesto of PPP. Besides, Roti, Kapra and Makan were a very big incentive. Zulfiqar Ali Bhutto, the chairman of the party was my favourite leader, especially after he returned from Tashkent negotiations after 1965 war.

During the 1971 elections I was magnetized towards PPP and I had no hesitation to vote for the party and also persuaded many of my friends to do the same. PPP came out victorious in West Pakistan. It was beyond expectations of many people, however I wanted to explore further if I could continue my attachment with this party after my retirement.

Time passed very quickly and we lost East Pakistan in 1971 war. That was a very big tragedy and the entire nation had to undergo a big emotional shock. This was the first time a common man raised finger against Mr. Bhutto for the loss of East Pakistan because of his personal interest. However this was set aside due to Bhutto's taking over the government and pulling strings here and there to neutralize this set back. Our People are generally shortsighted and they soon forgot about this chapter for political complacency.

PPP never the less, started coming out in its real colours. The first action was to brush off the poor devotees and replace them with the feudals and dirty influentials. Because of this the first casualty was Mr. J Raheem, known to be the real author of PPP manifesto and the then secretary general of the party. He was beaten up and tortured by Mr. Bhutto's cronies and thrown out of PPP and I think he lost his life due to this shock.

The second was loss of discipline. The PPP workers were so driven and directed by the rogue and vagabond elements that they literally took over the industry and forced the owners to dance naked in front of their officers and workers. The result was that most of them left the country and their industries were nationalized and ruined. Nationalization was the third and vital casualty which really destroyed an up coming industry and all other foreign investments. Even the small private schools were nationalized. In a nutshell all the existing infrastructure of the country was destroyed beyond repairs by the so called "JIALAZ". It, of course took a long time to recover through denationalization by subsequent governments including Benazir's one.

With the passage of time PPP government became more and more oppressive and started creating harassment in public. Any one who opposed Mr. Bhutto had to be treated as enemy of Pakistan. Some of the founder members of PPP like Iftikhar Tari and others were put in Delai camps in solitary confinements to learn the lesson of obedience. People like Maulvi Tufail Muhammad, chairman Jamaat-e-Islami were put in jail and treated so disgracefully that he could not describe the humiliation he was made to undergo. People of course knew the details which cannot be expressed in civilized terms here. Killing of Doctor Nazir Ahmed and Khwaja Rafeeq was also part of the same campaign.

The last performance was introducing official rigging by the highest party authority in the 1977 elections which brought **PNA** into action against them and ultimately martial law by General Zia-ul-Haq.

However one big credit goes to Mr. Bhutto that the party slogan Roti, Kapra and Makan reached deep into the roots of the poor people so madly that even today the leaders of PPP are enjoying the fruits of that slogan, without providing any credible benefit to the poor people.

The second round of PPP began with Benazir in 1988 and 1993 taking over as prime minister of Pakistan. She started of well but after marriage with Zardari in 1989 there came a reign of corruption and Zardari became so much involved in every government deal that he earned the name of Mr."10 percent" in Pakistan. People at large resented this but it didn't make any dent in Zardari's and Benazirs's determinations to continue corrupt practices. She was ultimately dismissed by her own party's president Mr. Laghari in 1996. Zardari is now the president but unfortunately one cannot dispense with his bad reputation with the noble appointments. It goes with him and follows him everywhere to UNO, America, China or Europe.

People Party should be thankful to Gen. Musharaf who ultimately bailed them out through 'NRO' under some agreement best known to Musharaf, BB Shaheed and Bush.

MQM (Mahajer Qaumi Movement) later turned to (Muteheda Qaumi Movement) is the next awami party having roots in the poor and middle class society and was indeed liked by the people. It started of from Sindh but before it spread over to rest of Pakistan it fell into the hands of oppressive and rogue elements who started plundering and robbing affluent people to build up party funds. They also levied forced subscriptions on general public which spread a wave of terror in big cities like Karachi, Haidrabad and Sukher. People really felt hostage to this element and none of the educated party members had the courage to leave the party. Most of them started enjoying the funds collected and supporting such rogue elements to punish people illegally by creating no go areas with torture cells where no lawful authorities could have an access. At times the Army had to be called to rescue people from these cells and torture houses. Some of the criminals and accused ran away and settled in foreign countries by establishing the party secretariats. Since then the party chief, Mr. Altaf Hessian is living in London and is commanding the party from there.

Initially I thought this party had a great potential because of its appeal to common man but its leader getting involved in criminal activities restricted its orbit only to Sindh. The party is controlled by a man sitting in London. I therefore call it a "remote control party" (RCP) rather than MQM. He has no courage to come and face the people in Pakistan. He addresses them on telephone depicting a pathetic scene where the in country leadership and the crowd sit and listen to his sermons very obediently. It indeed presents a scene of people from graves with spiritless bodies listening to the voice of a spirit from the other world. No one has the courage to question his authenticity. The leader, who cannot come and sit physically and share compassions with his people about the problems they are facing, has no right to lead them sitting thousands of miles away from Pakistan. If he is scared of his personal safety how can he be trusted with the safety of his people? Imagine a commander in chief sitting in enclosed protected bunker for fear of being kidnapped by the enemy.

ANP is a regional party restricted to frontier province only. It had a great reputation of being a party of principle and courage but lately has shown an instinct of greed and cowardice while facing crises in Pakistan. The leadership did not come up to its reputation of courage and principle. I only hope it regains its past glory and honour that its founder leadership had possessed.

Jamat-e-Islami is a party of religious values and it applies rigidly these principles in politics. The best thing is that it belongs to poor and middle class people and has the distinction to practice equal treatment for everyone, honestly and boerd. Unfortunately it has the reputation of collaborating with dictators and subsequently supporting them for ruling the country. I feel this was more of impersonation rather than the reality. However they need to vowel away this dust associated with them. Their strength lies with their religious values and I feel that is their asset.

People in Pakistan though perform all religious rituals rigidly but majority remain naive about the real spirit of Islam. Jamat is also to blame for their lack of approach to a common man on the street. Their membership is so stringent that very few people can achieve that standard. I remember, soon after my retirement a local Jamat Amir came to me for a help in the elections. I told him I was not accepted as member in your party, why should I support you. He had no answer but I wrote a big letter to Qazi Husain Ahmed requesting him to let sinners like me come to your fold. With your good company and association I may change and improve. Soon after, I saw some relaxation in the party membership rules.

I am not member of the Jamat but I personally feel that if one day Jamat gets an opportunity to rule; this country will be made.

Muslim league, the founder party of Pakistan was once the darling of the people but a few years after Pakistan's existence it split away into different factions and became one of the weakest parties of country. Muhammad Khan Junejo in 1985 and Mian Nawaz Sharif put some life in this party in 1992 and made it again the front runner in the country. Nawaz Sharif with his professional approach and good governance brought Pakistan industrially competitive and politically stable country in the region. He also has a privilege and honour to make Pakistan a nuclear state inspite of pressure from the entire world against him. Pakistan became the first nuclear state in Islamic world which gave her recognition as a distinguished Muslim country in the world. The most important was that India started looking at us as equal power in the area. This was one of the reasons which brought Mr. Wajpei, the prime minister of India to travel by Bus to Pakistan and first time accept Pakistan a reality, under the shadow of Minar-e-Pakitsan in Lahore.

General Pervaiz Musharaf put a stab on the back of Muslim league, the party which elevated him to the chief of army staff. He almost destroyed this party by making the main faction dormant for eight years but supporting a dead horse like Chaudhry Shaujat and Pervaiz Ilahi for as many years. However Mian Nawaz Sharif has again put some life in the party to enable her to at least start moving like a snail but hopefully with public support it may start running to catch up with PPP very soon.

Tahreek-e-Insaaf is a new and small party but by principle the strongest party in Pakistan. Imran Khan, the party chairman is the most out spoken, straight forward, honest and brave leader. He believes in straight politics and dislikes dubious dealing with the innocent people. He has fairly good experience in welfare activities and has practically demonstrated his concern for poor for his contribution of "Shauket Khanum hospital" and "Nammal University" in Mianwali are examples that no other political leader has so far matched with him.

His politics is honest and Chinese style, talk straight and say what you mean, unlike some of our leaders who think politics is something very difficult and crooked and more they lie the more they qualify as good politicians.

It was my endeavor to bring a neutral view of all the prominent political parties to the common man to understand, analyze and then chose for whom to vote in the next general elections whenever they take place. Their opinion may not bring any change in the country in their lifetime but is bound to effect their next generation whose lives will depend upon how intelligently and honestly you put the country in the right hands. Please be kind to your children and their future for an honorable place in the world. This might be held as one of the reasons for your forgiveness on the Day of Judgment.

I have deliberately left a few small regional parties because they have no over all impact on the country's politics and people's social structure.

Provoking a change

A Noble Vision

4ᵗʰ December 2008

Barak Obama's reference to change! Endorsing: "yes we can", was his slogan during the election campaign. It basically came out of his determination, willpower, sincerity of purpose and above all to change the world for a cause that dreams of human excellence and accomplishments. He is now the elected president of the United States, the first black candidate who swept the polls more than any white could have achieved. His competitors paid a very rich tribute to him on the victory and offered all the help and assistance in running the country. The change that he had pledged is no doubt a craving that the Americans and many other people of the world, specially the world of poor and deprived like Obama's own roots had realized.

The change does not come by change of the colour it comes by changing the mentality, the concept, the character, and above all the convictions and the feeling for each other irrespective of nationalities. Poverty, racism, and injustice should be the common cause to fight, instead of the religion and ethnicity. Americans and Al Qaeda should be ready to sit and eat at one table, discuss and bridge the gap created through misunderstanding and clash of views. Similarly American and British must revaluate situation with Iraqis instead of looking for an excuse to extend their stay. Respect for each other's sovereignty and independence instead of signing a recent pseudo type agreement between their governments for staying in Iraq until 2011. There could be no real agreement between a victor and the vanquished. Both parties have to be free and at the same level to realize such a contract.

Americans must learn to respect Iranian views on common controversies. Issues can easily be set aside with mutual respect. If you make nuclear weapons you certainly need plausible efforts to forbid others to do the same. Allowing Israel an easy access to nuclear approach and disallowing the Iranians the same technology and favour is by itself a weird notion. Obama must ponder about this and really

85

think of a change with judicious conduct, vision, and equality for everyone where you could indeed substantiate the change "yes we can", otherwise it will be forgotten and backfire as an election gimmick and duplicity used by you for achieving your goal. Ideal situation is though impossible to accomplish, yet one can fairly come closer to the objective acceptable to meet the expectations and hopes of many. Gone are the days when people enjoyed killing people on territorial conflicts and religious differences. The world has reached the climax of civilization, education and advancement. Our leaders have to change and sort out the differences on dinner parties rather than in battle fields. If we follow the old style of settling feuds in arenas where barbarians forced their heroes to face the wild animals for winning or losing, we will not be entitled to have the status of a highly civilized society. There is no use of exploring the planets, Mars, Venus, or Jupiter for future resources and living hopes if we are going to play the same game as we are doing on this mother Earth.

I don't care what colour Obama possess, what religion is he practicing, and what habit is he enjoying; he has reached a peak of his career by becoming the president of a super power which is economically and militarily leader of the world. A real leader is one who takes his victory a challenge to work for his people's welfare and takes pride in bringing peace and prosperity for those under his domain. Try his best to improve relations with neighbours. Unless you are welcomed in neighbour's house how can you expect a red carpet treatment across the Atlantic. Your understanding at home certainly provides easy access and greetings from outside.

The black man as president of United States may have, at times a kind of embarrassing moments and an inward fear when he has to prove it to white colleagues that he is as fair to his own colour mates or other underdogs as anyone else. He may not have this reservation but if he feels so, he has to get rid of these feelings. I am saying this because of my personal experience on visits to America where I always forgave a black official mistreating me to show off his white colleagues for scoring some points on his performance.

How about a dream meeting with Osama Bin Laden to cool the environment to suit international peace back on Earth and save millions of people from everyday embarrassments in the United States and other countries. Osama might have been the cause of trade centre's destruction (not yet determined in any enquiry) and killing 3000 people. America has avenged almost hundred times more deaths in Iraq and Afghanistan, which should be enough to balance the account or make up for the loss and get even with all stake holders. I am sure Obama with the change that he vehemently cried can practically prove "yes we can". I know the existing systems and the masters of those systems will not let him approach in this direction, however, even his one step towards this direction will be remembered as an international reformer with more respect and honour than any other president of the United States.

America is not entirely to blame to upset everything in the world; Al Qaeda, Afghanistan, Iran, and Iraq also have to share the blame. They must all play their part to bring change in their behaviour to normalize the situation. However, the history shows and day to day observation reveals that it is the stronger who has to initiate to give up the coercion on the weak and untenable in the first place and then expect some kind of trade-off from the weak.

One far reaching affect of the change that I personally and majority of the people and deprived expect from Obama is a new world order of cooperation that could bring the people closer to each other and develop a sense of partnership. He may not be able to bring an ideal situation but he can certainly initiate improvements so that a change is actually felt throughout the world.

It is often reiterated that with new scientific technology the world has become a global village, but what kind of village where nobody knows anybody; neighbours don't recognize each other and are ready to pounce and kill each other with slight misunderstandings. You don't let your village mates enter your street without visit visa; don't let the hungry eat food which is surplus to your requirements that you may throw to animals but deprive your fellow beings to use for their survival. Yet you claim to be living in a village called the global village. We have also seen the people of the same faith not allowing each other to practice and join the prayers without visa. Look at the Muslims where the Arabs don't let them enter Mecca without visa to come and stand together for prayer. What kind of brotherhood and spirit you can inherit with such a frame of mind. It is indeed a shame village if at all you like to call it a global village.

The first item on agenda for change should be the elimination of terrorism. The seed of this deadly disease was sown by the west themselves. Hitler was the first to use it as Holocaust of the Jews. After World War II, the British transported it to Palestine and then the Americans took over and supported it to be used against Palestinians. From Palestine it spread in the shape of Al Fatah, Hammas, and Al Qaeda and maybe Lashkar-e-Tayaba, many more small branches sprung up in many countries, mostly Muslims because they were the only one affected. Mr. George W Bush Jr crossed all the limits after 9/11 and made sure that the world does not sleep peacefully. He further extended it to Iraq, Afghanistan, and Pakistan. The change that Obama proclaims must stop this storm before it destroys the west and America themselves. The superpower needs to be fair and just in dealing with the nations irrespective of their size and America's personal interest. I think the key to peace is buried at Tel Aviv. It would be better to take it out and leave it in safe hands which would be better for Israel, Middle East and rest of the world. Closing eyes or supporting Israel blindly would be fatal for all the stake holders in the long run.

We have also seen American hegemony in terrorising small states and using them for their purpose, like "either you are with us or against us". General Musharaf of Pakistan was made a hostage to join in Afghanistan war. In fact Musharaf as a friend could have been more useful than a hostage. The whole situation would be different today if the principle of friendship and cooperation was adopted to assist America in those crises. The present catastrophe and wastage of immense resources which has brought United States to an economic collapse could have been avoided.

One area where I would like to see a change is the visa system to enable people to travel to different parts of the world to meet each other for better living. I remember Pakistan and most of the other third world countries did not need a visa throughout Europe and most of the other countries in the early and late 60's. There were no illegal immigrations and people freely enjoyed mutual respect and benefits. Crime was negligible amongst or because of the visitors. The more the restrictions were enforced the more crime was observed within the parent and the countries of the visits. God created Earth for everybody to go anywhere to explore the wealth of this Earth and generate new opportunities for better prospects of living for themselves and their communities. I am sure COLUMBUS did not take a visa from Red Indians to discover America. English pirates did not have a permit to enter Australia and New Zealand. America was a land of immigrants and let it remain so to be exploited and used for the benefit of the new entrants and for the present inhabitants. If the blacks had not come here who would have developed this land for you in that difficult and terrible terrain. It was those slaves who provided you the incentive to command and live well. If they had not come, Obama would not be here to take over as the president. He is now president of the blacks and whites, Asians and Hispanics and all the other small communities. They are all Americans and the entire populace is immigrant, some from other world to America and a few from America to the other world and ultimately everybody from this world to the next.

There is still so much of virgin land on these continents which can be exploited for the benefit of mankind for at least another two to three centuries but the selfish instinct that we have developed over the last few hundred years does not permit us to allow others to share the same comfort that the forefathers of the present rulers and elites had sought a few hundred years before. The world of today is looking for a change, the change that stops killing, terrorism, and committing excesses against their own fellow beings. Love, sympathy, and feeling for each other is the essence of civilization that we all talk so much about, to bring people closer to each other.

Mr. Obama it is a very big challenge! Can you do it; "yes you can".

Afghanistan turmoil favours no one

09th September 2008

Neighbour! He said, "Mind your own business, look after your own problems and troubles, which I can see are numerous and need immediate attention of every one of you to correct". He made it abundantly clear to me while sitting across the table in a restaurant at Peshawar. I wanted to be nice and patient with N Zee (Mr. N Z Khan) and continued conversation as a good neighbour. I told him that world was a global village today and living in the adjacent village it was my concern and duty to be of some service to you. I agree with you about our own problems and troubles, but in my opinion "Thy need is greater than mine". You are not only our next door neighbour but a brother in faith and we are dependent on each other in many ways. We drive about 1/7 of electricity from Kabul River and draw power and strength from your sympathy and solicitude during emergency with our eastern friends. Similarly your food, education and most of the trade with outside world flows through Pakistan. During the Russian invasion we used all our possible resources to fight and drive the invaders out of Afghanistan. We welcomed five million afghan refugees with open arms and even today three million are honourably living in Pakistan. We are doing all this as good neighbours and under the principle of a "friend in need is a friend indeed". You should also understand that most of our problems are outcome of your troubles. We didn't have such conditions before you got involved with Russians and now with Americans. So you also owe me an explanation and viable solutions to yours as well as our problems.

He felt relaxed and started narrating what actually happened to Afghanistan after the Russians left in 1989. USA and Pakistan left us high and dry without any subsistence and solid organization. The whole country was taken over by different groups of mujahedeen and warlords. Loot, arson, rape, and killing were order of the day. Pakistan along with Saudi government tried their best to establish a workable afghan government but failed in the face of local opposition from mujahedeen and warlords. The situation became so dangerously erratic, the peace was completely missing and people had started running back to Pakistan.

Taliban were indeed a very very welcomed arrival in that situation. We were not concerned who brought them but they came with a message of peace and justice. The warlords could not stand in front of their simple, upright, moral, and righteous approach and started disappearing. Most of the mujahedeen groups with a very little resistance surrendered and accepted the new rule. This was the first time we saw an era of peace and tranquillity in Afghanistan after a long time. The poor people took a sigh of relief from the cruelty of the mujahedeen and warlords. Poppy fields vanished completely and the whole world acknowledged the total disappearance of drugs from Afghanistan. The governments of Pakistan and Saudi Arabia recognised the new regime but the big powers like America, Russia, and England stayed away because they probably could not stomach peace in this area. They started planning to break down such a regime that was not willing to continue with fraud and criminal activities in the world especially in a strategic location as this. They started propagating Al Qaeda's existence in Afghanistan and create some distraction against Taliban without realising that it might one day land them in the same trouble themselves. This was not only the feeling of N Zee but his inner soul was crying along with the poor majority of Afghanistan.

Al Qaeda was a very small group of Saudi Arabian mujahedeen claiming to fight Israel for her excesses on the Palestinian people and undertook to strike Israel's interest where ever visible in the world, unless Israel stopped her atrocities in Palestine. Americans, instead of restricting Israel's human rights violations they got after Al Qaeda's intentions against Israel. As expected, this kind of treatment provoked Al Qaeda for an unwise attack on American embassy in Kenya in 1998 and subsequently a few attacks in Saudia against Americans. Those were the most unfortunate incidents which brought sudden increase in hostilities between America and Al Qaeda. A small irritant between Israel and Al Qaeda was escalated beyond proportion by America and Al Qaeda. Such misadventures happen when no prudent and rational approach is adopted by the parties concerned. However, the more educated and stronger must bear more responsibilities.

At this stage I provoked him on Mr. Hamid Karzai's role and his government's contribution in Afghanistan. He said, "He has taken six years to gain control of Kabul. In this proportion he may take another twenty years to reach Kandahar. He knows how to make fool of Americans. Let us talk about something more useful.

The horrors of 9/11 actually fell upon poor Afghanistan more than America. The government of Taliban and their guest Osama Bin Laden were held responsible for this heinous crime. The American government fabricated charges, which were beyond the capacity or capability of anyone of them. As a few observers quoted, they had to blame someone and take action to satisfy their own people, as a good cover up. That is how an honest and stable government of Afghanistan was destroyed. Their only fault was protecting Osama Bin Laden from handing over to America. That was part of their traditions and transgressing from it was the greatest dishonour. They offered to negotiate and even try him by international court in Afghanistan through any international guarantee. This was refused and an attack, already planned, was carried out by employing Northern Alliance against the advice and consent of Pakistan government. Gen. Musharaf of Pakistan supported the operation with specific undertaking that the attacking forces will not enter Kabul. This promise was blatantly broken and anti Pakistan forces were allowed to take over Afghanistan. Since then the war has spread over half of Pakistan without any end to be seen in the forth coming future. Pakistan is being adversely affected economically and politically and every new day is bringing more trouble and instability in Pakistan. How is it helping United States is not visibly known. Billions of dollars have been wasted and many more billions will sink in this well with no hope of sweet water coming out of it for USA. Barack Obama and John McCain may like to hold a mental exercise before a final presidential debate, to the American people.

I interjected at this point that America has no enemies in Pakistan, except in the tribal belt where they are engaged in fighting against so called Al Qaeda and Taliban. The locals there have the same characteristics, language, dress and lots and lots of sympathy for Taliban. This does not equate them with their enemies unless they make them so. However, to be honest America has no friends in Pakistan either. Those who claimed to be so have now been converted as either neutral or against; because of the American government's policy in the area. In fact even when they were standing with our enemies, many in Pakistan regarded it as American compulsions to fit in the overall world politics as a super power.

Unfortunately the Al Qaeda, or to be more appropriate the Osama Bin Laden game has been transformed into friend or foe game and everyone in Europe is also following the same philosophy as that of America. Of course those who are driving benefit out of it are happy to continue to draw the last penny of the dividend from the proceeds.

Let us put the so called terrorism, at our hindsight and get down to a fresh appraisal of the current approach that might bring a new dimension to the entire situation. The need to commence some kind of new dialogue with a few disparate and desperate may work out towards better prospects. It is not something out of the blue but who knows who can click and turn back the clock. The present path does not seem to be going anywhere except in a dark tunnel of a time machine where the American people and their friends would not wish them to follow. We in Pakistan being an American ally have the same feelings and would not like to escort them to that end. Much of the dollars have gone to dust, let us utilize the left over for the welfare of the people of this region and make them affluent to stand in line with America through every thick and thin. I sincerely feel that there are a few who could help lead to an appropriate path, following which is still their own prerogative. Take it or leave it is still an option and may be worth a try for good of both sides.

N Zee and I kept sitting and talking about who will bell the cat till the waiters called it a day and we got up lest we were shot by Taliban or security forces. However, we were still hungry of the specifics and shifted to his new house at Hyattabad. It was difficult to reach a conclusion in such a situation but we both agreed that the solution lies with America. NATO is only like a faithful dog and is performing well. Pakistan's new government and her new decision making leader, Mr. Zardari cannot be trusted by either of the parties, Americans or Taliban/

Al Qaeda. The large no of people of Pakistan, also have no confidence in him because of his past characteristics.

We talked a lot and left most of the things inconclusive because he said, Neighbour! Let us lay off from Afghanistan because unless a few accountable and responsible team up together to repair, the current situation may perpetuate in our lifetime and what happens after that is irrelevant to us.

Putting Pakistan against the wall

16ᵗʰ December 2008

9/11 tragedy was so severe that the American president Mr. George W. Bush junior lost his nerves and behaved like a wild lion mistreated by some of the people in the arena. He immediately threatened to launch a crusade against Muslims. We, in the third world countries always looked at the super power as our leader in all aspects of life. We had an image of a leader leading the world and not a person who deems to think after the action where the damage is already done. We always thought that in a super power every conflict or issue undergoes such an extensive scrutiny that there is no scope of any misadventure. Unfortunately it did not happen in this case and the super power failed to provide a good example this time.

Afghanistan was the first victim of the 9/11 episode, where Osama Bin Laden, the so called master mind in this operation, was hiding. The air attack to kill a few perpetrators came with such a wrath and vengeance, which the world had never before seen such a high intensity carpet bombing and new weapon display. It was followed by a ground assault by Northern Alliance and allied forces that along with the destruction of the country's infra structure at least fifty thousand civilian men, women, children were killed. Force of a few thousand Taliban escaped here and there with no resistance shown on the ground. Kabul was captured within two to three days of operation. Till today after seven years, the operation stands still with day to day fighting of Taliban and allied forces with guerrilla warfare tactics and off and on suicide bomber attacks by the Taliban guerrillas. The return of Afghan refugees from the previous Russian war was halted and Pakistan kept suffering under the burden of these refugees, besides crime and terrorism so created because of them.

Pakistan was forcibly made part of this operation against their neighbour. The coward ruler of Pakistan, Gen. Musharaf, scared of going back to stone-age joined the coalition against Afghanistan. He succumbed to pressure and became part of the war against the wishes of the people of Pakistan; otherwise there were many other ways to control this storm.

This was a great shock to the people but they accepted this unholy alliance and worked with American friends with all sincerity to succeed in Afghanistan. However, the attitude of Mr. Bush during visits of India and Pakistan in the year 2006 was seen very humiliating by the people where civil nuclear cooperation agreement was signed with India and cricked coaching and playing session along with do more lesson was given to Pakistan. This discriminative action from a friend was watched with grief and sadness by the people of Pakistan.

Pakistan became the warehouse of the logistic support of the NATO forces fighting in Afghanistan. A few airfields and a complete terminal at Karachi airport was handed over American friends for success of their mission. One hundred thousand Pakistani troops were employed in the tribal area of Pakistan to stop any flow of Taliban fighting against the occupation of foreign troops in Afghanistan. This was the first time in history of Pakistan to deploy their army in the area against the established agreement between the tribal belt and government of Pakistan. It was greatly resented by the tribal's, which gave rise to a kind of rebellion in the entire Fata region. This resulted in the killing of local people by Pakistan army and reciprocally our own troops by the tribal's. About two thousand army personal and many thousand civilians have been killed so far. At least one million local refugees migrated from this region to internal areas of Pakistan. This was another very serious blow to Pakistan government for supporting this operation.

Do more philosophy of American friends forced Pakistan to commit more hostile acts generating more resentments amongst the tribal's. The wave of these clashes spread over to Swat state, the most peaceful area of Pakistan and home of tourism, stopping complete tourist industry in Pakistan. More army troops were deployed to fight the insurgency created due to the same cause. The war is going on with our own people and Pakistan is suffering economically and loss of life, above all the hatred which is irrecoverable for a very long time to come.

The use of drones by American forces against the tribal area extending to the government controlled areas in Banu, has added more fuel to fire. More hatred, more enmity, and more tension seem to have escalated and getting beyond the control of Pakistan government. It is also becoming more frustrating for the armed forces of Pakistan. The Pakistan Air Force is the target of this humiliation where people have started raising fingers on the capability of the PAF, which is being maintained with a very big burden on the tax payers. The Air chief had to confirm to the nation that Air Force could easily intercept and destroy these drones but for the restrictions imposed on them by the government of Pakistan. The people are feeling more irritated against American. The army feels bitter when for the sake of one person ten people including women and children are killed because of drones attack. This is no collateral, it is catastrophic.

Mr. Gordon Brown, the UK Prime Minister during his visit to Pakistan on 14th Dec'08 announced at Islamabad that most of the terrorist attacks in UK had its origin in Pakistan. It may indeed be true because Pakistan has been made the victim of this menace by the west themselves.

Now came the Bombay burst, another so called 9/11 labelled by India. Who planned and executed, is up to the intelligence agencies to find. A simple brain like myself finds it purposeful scheme after going through the entire episode. If one construed Pakistani idiot who might have been paid by RAW or CIA to affix Pakistani involvement for any future exploit or blackmail, the government cannot be held responsible for this. Indian government should not start running to find the details in Pakistan without looking inside under their own carpet. The more disturbing were our own American friends playing in the hands of Indians to support their game.

Let me be very honest to tell our friends that from Fata area neither it is possible to stop people from going to Afghanistan nor coming from there to Pakistan. It is not possible even for the entire ground forces of NATO countries to do that unless the people themselves are satisfied with the behaviour of our allies in Afghanistan.

Enough is enough! Our friends must realize the inner feelings and plight of Pakistani people undergoing this treatment for the last eight years. How long our friends and world think this stamina of tolerance would last. After all there has to be a limit of bearing and suffering. Our friends and the world must wakeup to realize that the collapse in all fields of endurance is approaching very fast. The sooner this situation is rectified the better it is for the entire world otherwise the end might result in a shoe shower to Mr. George W. Bush as a sign of parting respect, as done in Baghdad.

It gives me tremor to imagine if twenty to thirty million people are not manageable for the world peace and elimination of terrorism, how could one hundred and sixty million be managed if they are put against the wall. It is not a threat but a point to ponder for Mr. Barack Hussein Obama and our Indian friends also.

Mr. Bush and the Iraqi Shoes

23rd December 2008

A pair of Iraqi shoes has become a legend in American history. Never before has an American president been honoured with this kind of bouquet on his farewell speech. President Bush with great agility saved himself otherwise this unfortunate incident could have become a very serious event in the history of modern times. I hope and pray that this encounter does not establish itself a matter of tradition to future presidents of the United States. That might become a painful event for some serious Americans but a continuous humour for common public who really love Mr. Bush.

Iraq was a very peaceful country in spite of its dictator Suddam Hussein. It had, of course a very oppressive society but certainly not a destructive one. People lived in harmony and united without any internal strife amongst them. The majority did not like Suddam Hussein but wanted to remove him in an appropriate time with a peaceful transition that would not destroy their social structure and country's integrity.

Mr. George W Bush wanted quick time change to save the dear people of Iraq from this continuous torture imposed by Suddam Hussein. He appeared very fond of the people of Iraq because of their oil deposits and present oil revenues earned by them, which must be shared with American friends and brothers. He also wanted to establish good relations between Israel and the people of Iraq for stability and supremacy of Israel in the region. Iraq had the strongest armed forces in the area which was indeed an eyesore to Israel and my friend George W Bush.

Mr. Bush was looking for the weapons of mass destruction, which could be dangerous for America and Israel. He ordered to position a few rickety pickety vehicles in the desert and directed Mr. Collin Powell, his foreign secretary to brief the UN Security Council the very lethal and dangerous weapons hidden in those vehicles and underneath. The secretary made a good case out of these vehicles and also managed to authenticate it through the IAEA. The UN Security Council, which was eagerly waiting to put their thumb impression to start the proceedings against Iraq through arms twisting by USA, passed the resolution 1441 (8th Nov'02) to attack Iraq.

Iraq was invaded by American, British, and some other allied troops on March 20th, 2003. They destroyed their Air force, Navy, and civil structure completely. Then came the Army ground attack, which occupied the country after neutralizing the minor resistance offered by the Iraqi forces.

After the occupation and all the destruction done by the allied forces it was revealed by the same group that discovered the weapons of mass destruction, about the nonexistent of these weapons in Iraq. Mr. Colin Powell uncovered that conspiracy by accepting that the information provided was fake. He apologized to keep his conscience clear and resigned from this job.

To compensate all this folly a new plan was devised to establish democracy for the noble people of Iraq and get hold of the dictator to try him for all the atrocities committed by him against his people. The people of Iraq were disgusted on this kind behaviour of the coalition and revolted against this good gesture of their friends, America and the UK. At least four thousand Americans and two hundred and eighty British along with four hundred thousand Iraqis have been killed in this uncalled for war of cock and bull story. The Iraqis lost almost everything, the Nationhood, faith, unity, and discipline, but the allies lost their honour, unaccountable financial loss and all the moral values they ever possessed.

Mr. Bush's farewell visit to Baghdad was in fact in his views seeking appreciation for the good work in Iraq and its people for the last five years. The disgraceful treatment with Iraqi prisoners at Abu Ghraib, the atrocities at Fallujah and cruelties at Najaf, Karbala, and Baghdad were the main features of his performance. At the farewell press conference, the reaction of a journalist, Muntazir-al-Zaidi was not unexpected. The shoes parade, probably at first hypnotized the entire hall and before anybody could wakeup he had already showered two shoes of "size 10" on Mr. Bush as an award for his favours to Iraq for committing the above task. This has now become the part of history ascribed to America. This credit alone would have made Mr. Muntazir-al—Zaidi eligible for the award of man of the year for the prestigious magazines like weekly TIME or News Week. Mr. Bush also received honour awards as man of the year for 2002 and 2004 by the TIME and News Week. The criteria for 2002 are understandable but there was no substance and moral fibre for the award for 2004 because of these attributes of Mr. Bush. The magazine messed up their own name by awarding man of the year to an undeserving person of dubious character even if he was the president of the United States.

Mr. Bush ruled United States for eight years. His predecessor Mr. Clinton had left the country in and excellent state and standing in all respects. He left a very balanced budget surplus of $42 billion and the country with a promising picture all around. After eight years rule Mr. Bush has turned that budget surplus into a TRILION DOLLAR DEFICIT. The America at war with Afghanistan and Iraq, Pakistan in a semi war conditions, and trouble with terrorist from within and outside the country. American people; a symbol of hatred in the world. Curse of 9/11, cause of which is one of the mysteries of Bush's legacy. Perhaps the worst situation of leaving the country of world proceeds into bankruptcy.

The Iraqi journalist Mr. Muntazir-al—Zaidi though made a history by hurling his two shoes on Mr. Bush, but it was actually the privilege of some American citizen from Washington D.C to confer this award on Mr. Bush for the deeds or misdeeds deliberated on the American nation for the last eight years.

I am sure Barack Hussein Obama must be taking note of these very small but extremely important incidents of national and international values. We all hope that the people will reconsider the quality of awards intended for the rulers of the super power and other countries in accordance with their accomplishments.

Justice for Benazir and the people themselves

27ᵗʰ December 2008

I am personally feeling sad about what happened to Benazir on 27ᵗʰ Dec'07, especially so when it happened in my city, Rawalpindi. Not only me there must be thousands of people who are burning from inside with the same flames of feelings. Unfortunately we are now used to bearing such sadness as a nation and if I go back in our earlier past; we are confronted with this kind of anguish as a religious background. We did the same with Imam Hussain (p.b.u.h). Our brothers and friends called him from Madina and deserted him in the desert killing him without even providing drinking water.

In Pakistan, we did the same with our first Prime Minister, Liaqat Ali Khan, at the same venue and place as Benazir. We cried a few days and then forgot about it as an act of destiny. In almost similar manner we killed Mr. Zulfikar Ali Bhutto. It was though a murder trial attributed to him as an accused but we have now come to the conclusion that it was a fake trial and was meant to kill him under a legal curtain.

Zia ul Haq went the same way. The majority did not like him, so made nature responsible to get rid of him. Never the less it was a murder. Come to think of it we even killed Quaid-e-Azam, the founder of this country by putting a serious patient like him in a third class ambulance that broke down from the airport to the Government House. A Governor General and the founder of the nation was provided the replacement of that rickety vehicle after forty minutes. Somebody must have been held responsible for this.

How many more murders and killings are we going to concur with? When we mourn all this, the nature smiles at us as a crowd of hypocrites who commit all tricks to kill them and cry louder to show it to the majority of the simple uneducated fools to convince them that it was indeed God's will to receive them as Shaheeds. The credit of Shahadat is bestowed upon them as a favour by all of us, and for most of them a mausoleum and Fateha for all times to come, as a compensation for their services to the nation and the people living in the country.

All I wanted to ask, "Is this the only duty we are left to perform in their remembrance". Are we not responsible to find the murderers and bring them to justice so that when we salute those Shaheeds for their noble and good deeds; we should also put a continuous curse on those who were responsible for taking those immortals away from us. There maybe a few invisible amongst the guardians of those Shaheeds who committed this heinous crime themselves and running amongst the real mourners with crocodile tears in their eyes.

I will not go as far as Imam Hussain (p.b.u.h) because we have all accepted it as God's will and feel that crying and Peetna is the only favour we could do to him and ourselves. 99% of us never pay a heed to what he laid his life for and follow those principles.

Pakistan is my subject of today's paper. Quaid-e-Azam went away; we never put a finger on those who were responsible for that fiasco. Let us pardon them all because the country was new and poor to afford good ambulance and systems. Let ignorance be bliss for those guilty of this crime. I am sure Quaid-e-Azam would also forgive them for his continues illness and old age.

Liaqat Ali was murdered in day light and within thousands of his followers. The murderer was caught and killed to wipe away the evidence. However, the planners were alive and some of them amongst the mourners. Most of the ruling elite knew and some of the public was quite sure about the killers but we all as a nation closed our eyes and conscience to live and not get in trouble ourselves. This coward mentality and logic saved those criminals to continue ruling us and commit the same crimes again. Liaqat's murder went in vain and only his 'Yaddein' remain with us.

Bhutto was the next victim. We all knew it was a fake trial by fake judges appointed by the dictator. All leadership of PPP and other political parties shut their eyes to live with the views that good days might come. Believe me good days are not a product of fear and cowardice. Freedom only comes with sacrifice and courage. Today the same kind of judges are being protected and installed by the so called mourners and entire fake leadership of PPP. Muslim League may keep crying, these judges are the need of PPP to protect them from NRO and other future crimes that they have planned to commit against this poor and coward nation.

Zial ul Haq was a dictator and his followers did not have enough public support to find the truth about his death. Right or wrong, dictator or democrat, every human being has the right to expect a justice from those leaders who are left behind. Unfortunately those who were installed after him were the product of his killers and therefore the justice went down in the deep well or in a one way tunnel.

Benazir is the last victim so far. She was called to be killed. How she came is also a story by itself. The authors of this story did not send her to serve Pakistan, but them. However, she, through her own intellect visualized the crack in her previous decision and changed her stance, basically for herself and maybe for Pakistan. This direction was not suiting the masters, so they tried to finish her at Karachi on 18th Oct'07. She survived and continued her mission, whatever it was. She was unfortunately assassinated at the same place and in day light, like Liaqat Ali was killed.

Who have so far tried to uncover the mystery of her murder? Those who are enjoying on her earnings have thrown the ball in Scotland Yard and UNO's court. If the murderers are amongst the mourners, only we the nation of Pakistan can expose them to the public. The public unfortunately has gone mad and are after the rituals planned by the PPP leadership and the murderers themselves. Imagine the waste of man-hours and time wasted in every street and public places, travelling to Garhi Khuda Bukhsh by thousand of poor people whose children maybe going without food because of the absence of their guardians for such a long time, sufferings of those who get delayed due to traffic jam and those patients critically needing doctors attention. What is Benazir or the nation getting out of it?—Nothing!

I am not proposing not to remember our dear ones. We must mourn and celebrate whatever is necessary to remember the occasions, learn lesson and follow footsteps of those being remembered, but certainly not organize a 'mela' out of it to shun away the national time and money.

Who has gained out of these current commemorations? If PPP thinks they have; they must be living in fool's paradise. The only people who have profited are the print and electronic media with elaborate advertisements, by government and semi government organisations amounting to several hundred millions of rupees. This could have been utilized for the welfare of those very people who, with bare feet and bodies marched across to Garhi Khuda Bukhsh from every corner of the country.

The way to commemorate her Shahadat was to find the real culprits who planned and killed her, to put the appropriate judiciary in place, to try them and administer justice. Not to protect the criminals and to maintain the same type of fake judiciary who murdered Mr. Bhutto. Let the people revolt against such justice which cannot protect themselves and their loving leaders.

The Moral of Gaza Story

13ᵗʰ January 2009

Once in a month or two when I get up in the morning, a close by loud speaker cries out about a sudden death of a neighbour or a distant resident of the area to the people to attend the burial in the graveyard at a specified time. The friends and other residents of the area get together to arrange the burial and pay the last tribute to the deceased. I was wondering how poor Palestinians must be coping up at Gaza where at least one hundred men, women, and children are dying: with everyday bombing from air, ground, and sea. The number of deaths must be extremely painful and exhausting to bury their dead. They must be organizing large groups of people in different shifts to manage. I also wonder whether their killers, the Israelis realise such a situation and suffering by the relatives and friends of these victims.

My mind also goes back to 1940's when Hitler decided to punish Jews for their disloyalty to him and collaborations with his enemies. I am sure the Jews of that period must be facing the same problems as the Palestinians are facing today. I often wonder if the Jews of Israel remember those days of Holocaust. I am sure a few history books must be lying in their houses to remind them of those horrible days. There may be many old people still living to relate them the stories of atrocities confronted by them and their children, by Hitler's men.

To me the massacre in Gaza smells like the human remains in gas chambers which Hitler enjoyed during the days of Holocaust. Israeli leadership is committing similar crime, while bombing the defenceless Palestinians and killing men, women, and children. They are doing exactly the same as Hitler did to their women and children. They seem to have learned nothing from the Holocaust experience and are following the path pursued by Hitler. He was putting defenceless Jews to prison on their way to Gas chambers. Israel is surrounding the defenceless Palestinians at Gaza to commit the same crime in the same manner.

The main excuse for starting this operation was firing Hamas's few rockets to Israel. It would be surprising to note that no casualty has been reported because of these rocket attacks except a few injured, whereas 850 Palestinians, men women, and children have died so far and several hundred brutally injured through the bombing of Israel.

The shame is not only on Israel to use F-16 and Tanks on poor pedestrians or simple foot soldiers but on Americans who encourage and provide protection to the barbarians who are committing these inhuman attacks. The world is watching this Holocaust with none or very little concern. They think their duty is only to plan medicine, food and sympathy for the poor victims. Instead of punishing the criminals, they encourage them to continue. The United Nation's resolution has been made a mockery by Israel because of the explicit American and British support. I don't know for how long nature will be tolerating this savagery on his people. Let it be known that the longer it is, the severest will be the punishment in the end.

Israelis may have to have a new appraisal about their role. Power is not ever-lasting. It has been changing hands so much and at times so frequent that the human brain has failed to unfold this mystery. However, the friendship and piety has shown great attachment amongst human-beings where only trust and reliability counts in the long run. If six million are living amongst two hundred million around them, it is advisable for them to live as friends. They cannot afford to make enemies with such an overwhelming majority. It will show its strength if not today but maybe tomorrow or even after two hundred years.

People with awareness and genius keep an eye on their past history to review their future. South Africa was a country of Black Africans, ruled by Portuguese in the 15th Cen. It changed hands with Dutch and British to rule the poor black majority for centuries. The blacks suffered even the disgrace of apartheid in the hands of a handful of whites for a long time. Ultimately the majority prevailed but the intelligent minority compromised to live as equals and are enjoying the same status with more respect with the new collaboration and democracy. The British in India and Pakistan, the Dutch in Indonesia, and the Americans in Vietnam, and many others have left to leave the land to the original owners or decided to live with them as friends and co-developers. Today, due to communication, education, and advancement, the world has become a global village where everybody knows everybody and lives with each other as good and sensible village mates.

The United States and the British leadership have been responsible to institute criminality when the Jews were first planted in Palestine after World War II. They are unfortunately still at their back to continue the atrocities on the Palestinians. However, Israel has to themselves differentiate between what is good and bad for them and for their coming generations, to live in peace with the actual land owners. The people of United States, who could not share even the bus seats and lavatories with blacks, have today reconciled to live as equals with all equal rights. In spite of having a clear white majority, they had to realise the strength of slaves and give them the rights to sit with them as equals lest they lose the authority of command over them. Today there is a black president in United States. The British have accepted all people of Common Wealth to reside as equal citizens in England.

To accept ones mistake is a bliss and to plead guilty of one's crime has considerable allowance towards the judgement and punishment. The United States happened to apply this rule in Iraq and is ultimately leaving that country amongst the mixed feeling of hate and forgiveness from Iraqis. Time is the biggest healer and complete remission may be an option one day with Iraq. I personally think a pair of shoes thrown at Bush with spite, should be considered enough disgrace and punishment for all that the America had done to Iraq.

Immigrants to Australia and USA are now in full control of these countries and peace prevails everywhere with the original inhabitants. The USA and Australia have a unique position who despite annihilating the Red Indians and Aborigines are enjoying reconciliatory behaviour from this small minority. Palestinians have a different equation. They are in majority and Israel cannot afford to misbehave with them. They have to learn to live with them otherwise one day they may be exterminated themselves. Let the sleeping Arabs sleep and take it as blessing for you; but if you force them to wake up from their nightmare, there will be no place for Jews or their western friends in this part of the world.

Husni Mubarak, kings of Jordan, Saudi Arabia, and the defeated Iraq may not be there for a very long time to disregard the atrocities committed on their Arab brothers. Many revolutionaries may rise to ask questions about your occupation of the Arab land and such a gruesome behaviour. To avoid that eventuality it is advisable for you to devise a system to live as friends with equal rights and respect for each other.

That is the moral of the Gaza story!

GAZA—THE TURNING POINT

8ᵗʰ February 2009

The Israeli atrocities at Gaza have shaken the civilized world of today. People have seen with their own eyes how the defenseless people of Gaza were literally massacred by a highly advanced country equipped with the most modern weaponry provided to them by a super power. Their schools, mosques and civil structure were destroyed and leveled to the ground. The purpose was to punish them physically and in a manner that they are kept busy in rebuilding for the next ten years and remain backward with no chance to advance in any other walk of life and development.

Arabs are all very dear to Pakistan, but Palestinians have a special place in our heart. They were struggling to save their land from Jewish community while we were fighting the war of independence against British, at the same time. We won the battle and secured a new country "Pakistan" for Muslims of India while Palestinians lost a part of their land to Jews who were supported by almost entire Europe, after the World War II. The Europeans and Americans were engaged to get rid of Jews from Europe and plant them at the heart of the Arab land to insure that this cancer keeps Arab within the limits and under control of America and Europe.

We, in Pakistan like Arabs mainly because they are Muslims otherwise there is nothing much common between them and us. We feel good when something good happens to them and we get disturbed when they get into a distress through worldly or natural calamity. This is in our blood and we cannot get away with this feeling even if we tried to do that. This feeling is not only for Arabs but for all Muslims of the world. It does not mean that we are unconcerned about other people. We indeed have the same love and affection for all human beings, but Muslims hold special status and are considered as a family member due to dictate of our Holy prophet that all Muslims are bound in brotherhood. This was meticulously practiced during his life time and after, for quite some times but with passage of time this feeling has been unfortunately ignored and in a general sense diminished. This resulted in a drift towards a general breakup in Muslim world itself with different factions and sectarianism.

The oppressed and poor were equally dear to the holy prophet and were to be given no less status then the Muslim brotherhood irrespective of their religious and other social affiliations.

This kind of binding is not peculiar to Islam but equally true in case of other religions. The Jews have special place in their heart for Israel and almost every affluent Jew saves money yearly out of their income and sends it to Israel in some form or the other to benefit state of Israel and other Jewish organizations around the world. This is part of their unwritten religious faith. Similarly Jesus Christ's emphasis on many occasions to "love thy neighbour" has no less significance. It certainly does not mean to go and live with your neighbor but commands Christians to look after your neighbours and protect them from every difficult situation, be partner in their hardships and share their joys in good times.

Gaza was a perfect case to obey the Holy prophet's injunctions by the Muslim rulers around Palestine. Every one of them failed to comply with its very important allegiance and obedience. Some were scared of Israel's might even when they were equally powerful and Israel could not stand for a long confrontation with them because of its size and strength, others were afraid of American economic and support program. None were confident of their own power and resources. It was beyond their imagination that world at large could not hold off and progress without their support. Fear was taking all faculties away from them. They were more worried about their temporary set backs in lifestyles and luxuries.

Hugo Chávez of Venezuela was the first man to call his ambassador from Israel as a protest against international criminal violations. This was a brave and statesman like gesture by a third world leader living with in the firing range of the super power who claims to parent Israel.

Egypt an equally powerful country as Israel could not dare to act like Hugo Chavez. Husnī Mubārak was busy in diplomatic maneuvers to solicit Israel to stop killing poor defenseless Muslims of Gaza. He had unfortunately collected all friends of Israel to sympathize with the people of Gaza. The least he could do was to **sever** diplomatic relations and warn Israel of dire consequences for such a cruel action. Instead he closed the only out side corridor for them to shift the injured and hungry people of Gaza. We in Pakistan could hear the cries of women and children. I wonder how he could sleep listening to the cries of dying children next door. It was pity to see eighty million Egyptians watching six million Israelis killing Muslim women and children and destroying their property at Gaza. Where there is will there is a way. These very Egyptians conquered the so called invincible Barlev lines on Suaze canal with in six hours of attack on Sinai in 1973. Israel therefore should not be under any illusions about their strength and might.

Shame on Pakistan, a nuclear Muslim nation of one hundred and sixty million did not have the courage to condemn the Israeli aggression for the fear of American reprisal and stoppage of economic aid. I wish we had taken this chance to do away with American Aid which is only meant for the benefit of our rulers. It certainly would have been blessing in disguise for the people of Pakistan in the long run.

I personally don't like dictators but am missing Saddam Hussein who always stood for the cause of Palestine against American and Israeli collusion. This was one of the main reasons to eliminate him and destroy Iraq to guarantee Israel's security in the region. Rest all stories about weapons of mass destructions and establishment of democracy were nothing but pure deception as is known to the world today.

I salute thee, Mr. Tayyip Erdoğan for walking out of Davos Economic conference in protest against Israeli aggression. The indifferent world leaders would not even allow shedding tears on the helplessness of poor Palestinian getting rain of bombs on their soil and that also from their own soil. I also salute the Turkish people coming to welcome their hero from Davos. Turkey is basically a friend of Israel and has been trying to decrease the gap between Israel and some of the Muslim countries like

Syria and Pakistan. However Mr. Erdoğan ultimately concluded that enough was enough and it was time to call spade a spade.

Israeli leadership has also to ponder about their future. For how long they can count on American support and control of the world money market by Jews. They may not be mindful of the destruction they have inflicted on poor Hamas in Palestine, or Hezbollah in Lebanon. The nature might have to teach them the lesson one day to taste the same carnage that Palestinians have undergone through Israeli actions. They seem to have learnt nothing from the holocaust. I hope they stop acting like a fool who does not learn even from his own experience. The only hope they have is to solve the Palestinian problem through independent and truthful approach. They must get out of western hypocritical net. The Arabs must get their judicious rights and Israeli their legitimate position which should provide guarantee to both Jews and Muslims to live together as human beings without taking any dictation from outside to disrupt their lives.

In recent history the Muslim brotherhood obligation was practically demonstrated during Soviet invasion of Afghanistan in 1979. They all came from almost all countries of the world to help people of Afghanistan and teach a lesson to the then super power. The Soviets were so defeated that even the union was shattered and they were shrunk to almost half the size besides losing the status of a super power. Although it was achieved through American help and assistance but it must be remembered by all that giving weapons is one thing but giving life for a cause is another.

Gaza seems to be another indicator for Muslims to revive the spirit of brotherhood and binding, to wake up and unite against the common enemy wherever in the world. It may be a difficult task because of their coward and selfish leadership but awakening of the people in this new era may force them to make it possible. That also is the prophecy of the end of the world in some of the Holy books. It should, therefore be incumbent on all, rich and poor, mighty and weak to stand in friendship and harmony amongst each other to live and let others live. This is what Barack Hussein is striving to achieve as President of some of the finest people in the world but without any praiseworthy collective leadership available in America. Unfortunately Mr. Bush and party had driven USA to the point of no return.

However, whatever the aftermath, Gaza may prove to be the turning point very soon.

Long March is coming again

13th February 2009

I was visiting London in July'08. I wrote a paper with heading '*9/11 is coming again*'. The purpose was to provoke a sense of responsibility to trace the real cause to prevent recurrence of such a crime. Unfortunately those responsible intentionally got on the wrong track to find the truth. Half of the world got totally confused for the action taken by the affected super power. After six years I was personally irritated and wrote the article that if justice is not done, the crime is bound to return. Although there is no comparison between 9/11 and lawyers movement but the justice is the common issue in both the cases.

I personally tried to reach the press to record my opinion, I am not aware if it was approved for publication. However, my experience shows that most of the newspapers avoid publishing the whole truth. Half truth is merely their aim and they generally focus on people to draw their own conclusion. The governments are also happy to face the half truth and keep a narrow corner open to escape under a slight ambiguity.

In Pakistan the long march by the lawyers community backed by the civil society is coming again because the first one was not provided the justice it deserved, by the government. The first march was very successfully combated by the government in defeating the justice in that battle; however the war is still on and we all know that winning a battle is not a guarantee of winning the war.

The first long march was attempted on 9th – 13th June'08, by the entire lawyer community of the country. It was indeed a massive movement of lawyers from Karachi, Quetta, Sukkhur, Multan, and Lahore, on one side and Peshawar, Abbottabad, DI Khan, Mianwali, and Mardan, from the north. All merging at Islamabad Constitutional Avenue to protest in front of the National Assembly building, as a show of strength to the sitting government to consider the legitimate demand of abolishing General Musharaf's illegal martial law order of 3rd Nov'07, which dismissed the Chief Justice of Supreme Court along with seventy other High Courts judges. The long march was successfully tackled by the government agencies and administration by sowing the seeds of dissention amongst the lawyers and the civil society in such a quick and successful manner that the whole demonstration dispersed within one day with almost no impact or pressure on the government. In fact it became more or less a joke with the administration when they successfully managed to wipe off the entire impression from the minds of the people like fading clouds after the heavy rain.

This was as big a movement as PNA's (Pakistan National Alliance) movement against Mr. Zulfiqar Ali Bhutto in 1977. It is very unfortunate that our government's culture does not accept and believe in peaceful demonstrations. They always want to see some action like in western movies or exciting series of events. Mr. Bhutto likewise did not foresee or even smell the storm coming after this peaceful demonstration till a few government buildings, offices, and cinemas were burnt and the army's refusal to fire at their own people. When he realised, it was too late. The movement had probably already reached the point of no return. After that what happened is part of our very dark and sad history known to us all.

Unfortunately we refuse to learn from our history because of our character and culture which takes pleasure in going against the lessons of history. This habit of going against the history has kept us behind and unmatched with other progressive nations. I sometimes compare Pakistanis and Americans the same way, with the only difference that America is too big in all kind of resources and has the capacity to bear small shocks. We are too small in everything to compete with them. However, Americans are heading towards the same destiny as ours if they continue in the same direction. It is heartening to see that at least there is something common between the two allies.

The second long march is due to commence on 12th March'09. The route and the rendezvous is the same. The government is the same but the advisors are different to further complicate the matter. I am sure they will not let the government solve this issue unless some destruction appears on the horizon. I have full faith in Mr. Sharif Uddin Peerzada, Farooq Naik, Latif Khosa, Malik Quyyum, and Salman

Tasir, the governor of Punjab to play their expert role to round off this government at the end.

The lawyers' peaceful intentions may not bear fruit against our historical background culture of excitement. However, victory for justice is the dream and vision which has to come at all cost if we have to live in community of the honourable nations. Besides, without the independent judiciary it is not possible to develop an incorruptible democracy.

It is the responsibility of the judiciary to dispense justice to the satisfaction of the people, otherwise these judges, the civil high and supreme courts and its buildings and huge infra structure are a big burden on the nation and country. Allama Iqbal (p.b.u.h) rightly said,

jis khet se dehkan ko mayasur na ho rozi

Us khet kay har khosha-e-gandum ko jala do.

This long march and *dharna* is supposed to be held in the shadow of this very expensive and graceful Supreme Court building. If "Me Lords" of this building do not provide the fair redress to the people's complaints and state affairs, you may interpret the above verse of Allama Iqbal in your own way and force a decision.

The last thing the lawyers community must remember that they cannot every now and then arrange such movements. This second time will also be a miracle. There is bound to be a decline in future attempts. Now or never is the choice. If you can successfully deal with the government you save and make this country, if you fail you break it forever.

A Judgement of Crisis

8ᵗʰ March 2009

All court judgements have a mixed feeling of acceptance and disagreements. Plaintiffs and defendants have the viewpoints which revolve around their personal rationale. At times some of these proceedings also become controversial in public understanding. However, when it apparently appear one sided, where intellectuals and common people, lawyers and learned start doubting its fairness there has to be something wrong in its credibility and truth. It is reasonable to hand over such verdict for public scrutiny and if the overwhelming majority of the people validate or endorse it either way, it should be accepted as credible. Law is made for the people and if the people do not agree to its legitimacy, it must be reviewed in totality. Reason is the spirit of law, when the reason ceases 'ipso-facto', the law also ceases.

The recent judgment to disqualify Mr. Nawaz Sharif and Shehbaz Sharif is a fit case for public scrutiny because this very law has undergone many changes to suit the ruling governments for disqualifying the opponents from their scheme of thought to favour rulers' personal agenda. The public opinion in this case is a must to purify and perceive the national view.

The judiciary in Pakistan has been under criticism since 1958 when the famous Chief Justice Muneer Ahmad passed the decree of the law of necessity in Pakistan. Since then all Supreme Court judges took shelter of this decree to legalise the action of every dictator who staged a coup d'état to over throw the legitimate government of the country. This one point agenda kept creeping in the roots of our judiciary and started eating away all the healthy tissues of this tree to really make it a complete *'TUND MUND' (bare)* at the end. It is a pity and I feel distressed to admit that our judiciary has come down to the level that today people openly declare to hire a judge than hiring a good attorney to fight their law suits.

Once before, in 1977 we tasted judgement of a Supreme Court in a murder case involving a very popular and revolutionary Prime

Minister, Mr. Zulfiqar Ali Bhutto, in a death sentence, which today is termed as a judicial murder. The party which became the victim of this judicial murder is today protecting and supporting the same judiciary for running their judicial jugglery in affairs of public and government affairs.

Another judicial murder of political career of two very important political leaders, Mr. Nawaz Sharif and Mr. Shehbaz Sharif was planned and executed by our judiciary of the same trait as that of 1979—on 26th Feb'09. The importance of both the cases is equally comparable as far as national interest is concerned. However, the most surprising and startling element is the attitude of the present central government which considers Mr. Bhutto's judicial murder as their ancestral case, least realizing, if that was wrong the present political judicial murder is also wrong and may be viewed in the same spirit. Otherwise the case of Mr. Bhutto may also be considered justified and filed in the same way on principle. What is good for you must be held good for others?

The significance of impartial judiciary is a point to ponder for all governments and people of authority. You cannot breed snakes and crocodiles and roam about freely in the farm without caring about your safety. It is good to have confidence in your own breed but certainly over confidence may be damaging and at times prove fatal when you are bitten by your own pets one day. A fair and impartial judge would always sacrifice for justice irrespective of his allegiance.

Mr. Churchill was an eminent leader who said and I quote, "if our judiciary is functioning, there is no fear of any defeat in World War II"; Hazrat Ali's (p.b.u.h) saying, "a state can survive under the regime of Kufur but cannot exist in a society of injustice", is as valid today as it was in those days.

A few glimpses of impartial judiciary has been a matter of pride and blessing in this country where the Supreme Court indeed proved to be a saviour of the country at a few critical moments like reversing a fraud of steel mill sell out by the highest executive authority of the country. In fact that was where the basis of current judicial crisis started. A few suo-motu actions by the deposed Chief Justice Iftikhar Muhammad

Choudhry, regarding missing personnel and misuse of vegetable farm houses has been a great relief for the affected people and state property.

The violation of constitution has been a very frequent crime committed by the rulers and men of authority where the handpicked judiciary kept her eyes closed and was ever ready not only to regularize the action but also provide more powers of amending the constitution. Probably that was one of the main reasons why there was frequent takeover by army and dictators. There has been four coup detat since the creation of Pakistan in 1947. In first three takeovers, dictators were satisfied with the regularization of their action by the parliament and judiciary but the last one by Gen. Musharaf demanded constitutional amendments and was granted willingly. If it continues with the same speed, the next coup could go as far as making their own constitution with explicit reforms in their favour and new form of governments.

9th March'07, was the first time a Chief Justice of Supreme Court refused to abide by the instruction of the dictator and created a situation where the lawyers and the civil society of the country openly revolted against Gen. Musharaf. Subsequently the Chief Justice was removed along with sixty judges throughout the country who refused to take oath on General's legal framework orders (LFO). However, unfortunately the new civil elected government backed the dictator turned president, to continue the same system and in the same fashion.

People of Pakistan have now decided to have an independent and impartial judiciary to dispense justice without any fear and shivers to the people and state of Pakistan. The lawyers community in its entirety are in forefront to help the people of Pakistan to have unadulterated justice to live a respectable life in the country. This seems to be the only basis on which the judgement crisis like the one created on 26th Feb'09 in case of Mr. Nawaz Sharif and Mr. Shehbaz Sharif could be avoided in future.

WHO IS THE CHIEF EXECUTIVE?

13ᵗʰ May 2009

Thanks to NRO which brought People's Party like a cloud burst in Pakistan before February 2007 election. Gen. Musharaf, late Benazir and Mr. Bush were the main architect of this ordinance which washed away many corruptions, murders and fraud cases of people's party and MQM leadership through this holly tenet. However the guilt hidden in their conscience could not be cleared and would remain with them as long as this government lasts. The basic aim was to make up the dwindling popularity of Gen. Musharaf with Benazir's political strength to continue American dominance and influence in Pakistan. On the other side Gen. Musharaf was keeping hundreds of prominent PPP defaulter's names in his pocket as a blackmail bargain chip to force a decision on Benazir.

After signing of the NRO Benazir ultimately decided to come to Pakistan but was surprised to see that the wind was blowing in the opposite direction. Her political acumen and flair changed her original stance at once which brought an unfortunate death to her. Pakistan indeed lost a big leader but the People's Party gained sympathy votes to come out as a majority winning party in the elections. She was gone but her husband Zardari took advantage of the boost provided by her because of this sacrifice. Her will, whether "ASLI OR NAKLI" (real or fake) kept the party within the fold of family but whether it helped the country was a big question.

Yousaf Raza Gilani was unanimously elected as leader of the house by all the parties in the national assembly. After the elections his first order as prime minister was to release all judges who were removed from their jobs and put under house arrest by Musharaf in Nov. 2007, when he declared the martial law in the country in his capacity as chief of the army staff. Everyone in the national assembly including the guest's gallery appreciated beginning of the parliamentary democracy in Pakistan. People thought that the seventeenth amendment would soon be revoked and democracy would be on our way to take charge of the country. In a little while there would be one chief executive and the tradition of authority being here and there would end and a fresh unity of command will take place for running the administration smoothly.

Soon after this, the PPP, as usual came back to its real colors and one after the other violated the written agreements with their coalition partner, Muslim league (n). This was seen by the whole nation on television. When confronted Mr. Zardari confessed and was glad to announce that it was done with intent because he thought it was not a Quranik injunction. His other promise of giving away his powers bestowed upon him through seventeenth amendment also went for a six (so far). By the way this was also announced in the joint assembly session in front of many foreign guests.

Mr. Gilani is a simple straightforward politician with apparently a good reputation and character. He is acceptable to a large segment of society and political parties. He is a man with good disposition and that is what we need to run this country. We really do not need a dubious genius for this purpose. He is internationally accepted and respected whatever he is. After all Prime Minister Junejo also developed his personality and became one of the most respected prime ministers in Pakistan.

Zardari also came with a bang. He was elected president with almost sixty seven percent votes from the senate, national and provincial assemblies. With seventeenth amendment in place, being chief of the peoples party he became the strongest president and informally the chief executive of the country. The prime minister's position automatically became subservient to the president like it was during the Musharaf days. I wish the popular people's party leadership had ascertained if Zardari was really worthy of holding all these political positions. Unfortunately none of the PPP leaders had the courage to raise any objection, including Peer Amin Faheem who disgracefully returned to grab the post of a minister.

A man is known by the reputation he holds and a leader, by the character he possesses and displays to his own people. His respect and reliability in the outside world is reflected by the respect he holds amongst his own people. Unfortunately, true or false Zardari did not have a very credible reputation and above board character in the country. The people he appointed like Farooq Naik, Baber Awan, Rehman Malik, Farzana Raja, Raja Ashraf and many others were all out to project him as saviour of the country and one of the biggest leader this country had produced. They were trying to portray him as saviour of this country and to some extent seem quite successful. I have no objection on their loyalty to Zardari because they have been appointed for this purpose and they owe it to him. My only grouse is that they also owe to this country which has taken the burden of bringing them up, provided education and opportunity to reach close to Zardari. Although Zardari tasted the fruit of their advice with Nawaz Sharif but unfortunately flattery is a very potent weapon to damage even a very strong person.

Now we must contemplate where Zardari stands internationally to deal with the world leaders for national interest and mutual benefit. Whenever a dignitary visits another country the concerned officials must go through the history of the visitor, his habits, character and reputation to discuss and deal with him appropriately. I bet they must be dealing with him in the style that he merits, especially so in one to one meeting where a great deal of off the record and understanding is verbally expressed and registered. I leave it to the imagination of our political leaders to speculate about Zardari's standing in the light of his reputation. When Obama says, just before Zardari's visit to USA that the civilian government of Pakistan is very fragile, one really cannot blame him.

Character is like steel that can break but never bends. It is not like lead that can be molded with every deal and threat. One time "KHAPPAY PAKISTAN" does not change a person's make up and integrity of the entire past. It needs life time endeavour to stand firm on principles at every extremities faced by a person.

The nation is confused as to who is the chief executive of this country, who has to deal within and outside with the world leaders. Irrespective of the regularization of 17th amendment, we thought once the president has pledged to the nation he automatically stands abrogated of his position of the chief executive. Mr. Gilani; we feel you are the chief executive on comparative values and the nation wants you to take over your responsibilities as such. You may as leader of the house initiate the constitutional changes. I am sure the law is not as blind as Mr. Baber Awan thinks and advises to the president. This situation of vagueness must seize if the democracy has to flourish in the country. Dealing with super powers should be your prerogative. Let us put an end to Gen. Musharf's follies.

During the current visit to United States Mr. Zardari took a lead as Chief executive. The nation, besides other things has strong reservations to his behavior and other expeditions, specially the MOUs of Indian/Afghan transit facilities through land route and his complete silence about the drone attacks to Pakistan. His taking Bilawal and presenting him as official delegate was not in accordance with any protocol decorum. Mr. Zardari must learn to function without the image of Benazir and Bhutto's spirit. He was unfortunately making joke of Pakistan by accompanying Benazir's picture at the United Nations forum before and now displaying Bilawal as legacy of Bhutto's at the official visit to USA. I don't know of any example before when a world leader keeping his wife's picture under his arm was seeking his personal recognition because of this.

Bilawal is an intelligent handsome young man who must be left alone to develop his own personality and rise with his personal merit, but not with his father's high position. Generally every father thinks his son is number one. This reminds me of an old story related by old grannys that an old time king asked his cleaner to bring the most beautiful child in his "derbar" the next day. The cleaner brought his own son to the king the next day. The king inquisitively looked at the cleaner, who said your Excellency to me he looked the best. I would request Mr. Zardari to end the hereditary politics. Let people come with merit. This would be his biggest service to politics of Pakistan.

With half and half chief executive sitting in prime ministers and president houses, one can hardly expect good governance in the country. This naturally sparks of loyalty/ disloyalty amongst the cabinet ministers and other government functionaries where most of the PPP ministers taking stride in standing shoulder to shoulder with the president and the other weak links bending towards the prime minister creating misunderstanding between the two of them. This results, most of the times very important decision's in lurch for a long time.

In order to stream line the administration it is vital to have one chief executive to run the country smoothly. I request Mr. Zardari to enjoy his five years presidential term as a ceremonial president, as is appropriate in the parliamentary democracy. This would be best for the country and Mr. Zardari to be more popular amongst his favourites and his own family members for the rest of his tenure.

"HUM KO SHAHOON SE ADALAT KI TWAQQO TO NAHIN

AAP KEHTEIN HEIN TO ZANJEER HILA DETE HEIN."

(Although we don't expect justice from the king's court, however if you say, we will pull the chain)

TALKING TO TALIBAN—A RIGHT PRESCRIPTION

24ᵗʰ May 2009

Today America and Pakistan are suffering from some kind of an unknown and medieval disease. It is though not infectious but certainly holds some germs of contagious nature. America spread this disease to Europe through social and defense pact contacts. Pakistan received this award through Gen. Musharaf's cowardice. The remedy of such an ailment lies in natural healing. Talking is a gift of god to cure this disorder. It guides human beings to understand each other, provides opportunity to exchange views, environments to come close to each other, wrap up all the bones of contention and explore the truth to live in peace and happiness. Forget and maybe forgive the excesses committed on each other because of misunderstandings. Find new path of reconciliation to commence lasting relationship between each other. Americans, Taliban, Pakistan and Afghanistan would surely benefit with this natural healing process.

It started with 9/11 when Mr. Bush contemplated that attack was planned and executed from Afghanistan by Osama bin Laden, the founder of Al-Qaida. He was in a hurry to show the lightning response to revenge from the culprits who dare attack his country. He deemed it necessary to win the sympathy of nation at this critical moment and convince them of American power to strike at the heart of enemy where ever he was, without delay. However it was silly not to realize its long term consequences on America and the world as a whole. Afghanistan and the then Taliban government were almost brought to Stone Age. The Americans are now paying through their noses to help Afghanistan recover or reconstruct from the destruction they had been responsible. I must however say that the major portion of this money is being spent on the revival or sustenance of Mr. Karzai and party instead of the people who suffered the most.

Pakistan was brought in this conflict under duress through her coward leader Gen. Parwez Musharaf. Instead of using Pakistan to revamp the situation and settle the feud, Mr. Bush forced Pakistan to become a party to war thereby minimizing all the chances of performing a mediator. The Taliban government, at that time was obliged to Pakistan for the help and recognition in the world. Mr. Musharaf didn't have the courage to disagree with Bush who was restless like a mad elephant. That is how we all lost an opportunity to solve a simple but a very emotional problem, and instead brought a very long drawn war in this region. Thanks to Dick Cheney and Rumsfeld who's contribution for this conflict would be counted no less than the Hitler in World War two.

Today it's not possible to retrieve the triggered arrow from the bow, but Mr. Barack Hussein Obama must hold his horse firmly and keep his stirrups tight to put an end to this horrible journey to a pleasant and acceptable end for all the parties. He is lucky to have better and more balanced team like Joe Biden and Hillary Clinton to assist him in this task as compared to Mr. Bush.

Pakistan can still play a very vital role in this conflict provided a diverse strategy is adopted instead of a customary routine technique of fireworks. We have followed this adventure for the last eight years and miserably failed to reach any sensible conclusion. Unless we diagnose the disease correctly we cannot cure the patient no matter how much sympathy we held towards him. I personally would request Mr. Barack Hussein to take solid steps even if they seem unpleasant to America momentarily. Accepting mistakes is bliss because it helps you improve your behavior and conduct. The way things are poised today it looks beyond U.S. government's power to settle this dispute. However there are very strong back door diplomatic avenues for a so called quick fix solution. Where there is will there is a way. There are people with common divine or spiritual faculty on both sides of Pakistan and Afghanistan to sort out the differences with logical Jirgah wisdom. I have been writing on this subject before and I am sure many others with equally painful emotions must be trying to do the same irrespective of what the war mongers and so called strategist think.

Today Barack Hussein holds the key to lock of justice and peace. He may have to use his own privilege as commander in chief of a super power to open the lock without any fear and prejudice for the sake of humanity and those who prayed day and night for his success in the elections.

The basic Taliban unit was the one who took over Afghanistan after the Soviet defeat and pullout from Afghanistan. They established a government which brought peace and justice on almost 90 percent of Afghanistan, eliminated complete poppy and drugs from the country. This was one of the reasons they received unqualified support from USA, Saudi Arabia, Pakistan and European Union. However presence of Al-Qaida, I think was the only impediment between the relationship of USA and Afghanistan.

9/11 created inordinate tension between USA and Afghanistan due to Al-Qaida's alleged involvement. Instead of utilizing Pakistan to neutralize Al-Qaida and keep control over Taliban for not inviting the war, and resolve the conflict between Al-Qaida and USA. It would have also helped finding the truth about 911 and punishing the criminals involved in that heinous crime, and also put an end to such an evil scheme in future. Instead Mr. Bush resorted to a war which resulted in destruction of Afghanistan killing of at least 35000 innocent men women and children 7000 American and allied personnel, 2000 Pakistani regular troops along with 10000 civilians. It has destabilized a large area of Pakistan and at least two million people displaced as refugees within the country. In the nutshell that one unit of Taliban has now grown to at least 40 groups with different names.

The main conflict started when 911 was ascribed to Al-Qaida and her care taker, Afghanistan. Instead of talking Mr. Bush decided to attack Afghanistan, the poorest country of the world, with all the modern weapons at her possession on one hand and under threat forced Pakistan to join the war as an ally. This put Pakistan and America in the same bracket and whatever chances Pakistan had for reconciliation was gone with the wind. Pakistan became as bad an enemy as America. Since then Afghanistan is under occupation of America. Although this occupation is restricted to a few prominent cities and airfields only. Rest of the rural Afghanistan is still under active control of Taliban.

We need America and believe me America needs Pakistan to save each other from the disaster where our crazy leaders have placed us. To get out of this mess the new leadership must take courageous and unconventional steps for the interest of two nations and world as a whole.

Before we talk about the situation of Pak—Afghan border I would like to remind the readers about the situation of American and Korean conflict, (1950-1953) When Gen. MacArthur requested an attack on China because all insurgency in Korea was coming through China. This request was refused by the men of wisdom at the white house. Imagine if it was allowed what would have happened to the world. A definite third world war was in the offing.

Pakistan and Afghanistan have a very long common and extremely difficult border which from centuries hold practically uncontrolled movement between the two countries. People on both sides have relations through intermarriages and other social dealings. Neither Pakistan nor Afghanistan have been in the position to control this voluntary relationship and movement between the people. even today the situation remain so and I think will not change for coming centuries. The point to be noted is that any outsider will have to face both the people irrespective of involvement of Pakistan and Afghanistan governments. Americans must face this reality and would be wise not to build fragile wall against such a strong natural bonds. There is no better advisor than British to seek help of this problem because they have been facing this for a very long time in the past.

To stop this self created catastrophe Americans may deliberate to vacate their occupation of Afghanistan as soon as possible. However if there are some other designs to stay, there would have other solutions to contemplate. Pakistan as I said earlier has great potential to assist in either case. Besides the government, there are people of wisdom and religious scholars to guide and help relieve this pain not only from Taliban but from Al-Qaida if there are still some remnants left.

Pakistan needs to tackle with the new crop of Taliban which has basically emerged out of the original roots of the Taliban government of Afghanistan. There may still be a chance to stop its growth which is good for both, Pakistan, America and maybe the world at large. With the passage of time this cancer might become incurable and a new research might be required for the remedy lest an uncontrollable disaster befall on the world.

Pakistan has been outrageously destabilized first time since its creation. It needs out of proportion help to come out of this self created calamity through American friends. Obviously the help therefore has to come mainly from America, and we are grateful that it is coming. However it needs to be arrested before it becomes a burden on our friends. We pray to save ourselves and our friends from this misadventure.

Talking is the only prescription which points towards the right substance and extract to cure this fatal disease that we had been led to with intent or otherwise. I appeal to our leaders and more so to Mr. Barrack Hussein Obama to come out with fresh slogan "yes we can"—meet this challenge.

AN OPEN LETTER TO:

BARAK HUSSEIN OBAMA

Provoking a change II

29 April 2009

Mr. President it was no less than a miracle we all attribute to your victory in the last elections of USA. Your slogan **"yes we can"** did bring a mini revolution in the minds of Americans. Your promise of a mighty change not only energized the Americans but the entire world of poor who incognito pinned hopes on your pledge and prayed from their inner self for your success. I personally think those invisible sounds of souls brought you in the white house which had always been the dwelling of a white elite and rich dignitaries since its built and holding of significance. I feel if Mr. Bush's order, sitting in Washington can raise storm in Afghanistan the very next moment, silent prayers can also change the destiny through the communion with the **god almighty.**

Your promise, I sincerely believe was not a winning jingle by hypnotizing the people's mind temporarily but a word of honor by America and where ever her influence extended. I, as a friend of America grabbed what I thought was good and you gave no choice but to accept your emotional perception. Whether you can now practically fulfill that pledge, is a challenge to your honor and office that you hold. If it has grown beyond your powers to prove, you may revise your pledge that everything is not possible to change but **"yes we will try"**.

I personally still respect your noble thinking which at least someone of your stature has unfolded for the people. This feeling was good enough for the elections for president because none else from your competitors could think of this. God may help you in fulfilling your promise even if people around you, I know are averse to your mission. I am sure people of your origin and the one you are commanding now, will be proud of you whenever your name would appear in books and references in dispatches, in your lifetime and after. At least I will tell my children and they to theirs that a man had come from a back ground of ignorance and brought an untainted light even to the most advanced civilization, the lesson that one does not have to only live for himself but for others who need it the most. This indeed was the message that my **Holy Prophet Muhammad** (p.b.u.h) had brought to the world and left it as a legacy for a few chosen people like you in the world.

The world peace may be your first objective. Peace would bring prosperity to America and elsewhere in the effected zones. **Iraq** has already been targeted on your agenda. At least this is what we learn from your plan, implementation of which depends on your government's conduct. **Seeing is believing!** We are all watching very intently. At least one million men women and children have been killed purely on ghost reports of WMD. Compensation may also be planned because this war was forced on Iraqi people through default of your predecessor. Loss of life they might forget but loss of honor is difficult to forget and forgive. Your outright repentance and apology might heal things for better future for both America and Iraq. Otherwise we all know that In spite of spending major chunk of your tax payer's money on, as you say the welfare and promotion of democracy for the people of Iraq, you earned nothing but shower of shoes from Iraqis at the end. It is good to be fair and straightforward instead of following diplomacy and duplicity.

Afghanistan is the most serious problem facing America today. Most of the NATO countries are also involved in this conflict. Pakistan of course is the front line scapegoat who is facing terrorism more than anyone else in the world. It started with Mr. Bush's itch to act in haste and anger in October 2001. Eight long years have seen nothing but escalation in terms of death and distress, depression and deprivation, and economic suffering all around the world. The haste and anger transferred nothing but hate and anger. Mr. President I pray you have the vision to peep in the past and seek new realities of future. Your so called down payment of 1.5 billion dollars to Pakistan will go as waste as so many billions of the past spent in Afghanistan. Pakistan has been destroyed because of American behavior and planning. Mr. President do not ruin America and destroy Pakistan. Move back from Afghanistan and keep away from Pakistan. Let them sort out their problems and in turn your problems. The ghost of Al-Qaida and Taliban are as unreal as was the ghost of WMD in Iraq. Following Mr. Bush is following the road to destruction. Some of your cronies are involved in mudding the waters. you may like to stop them or remove them if you are really interested to see the depth clearly. They are neither interested in America's welfare nor the security of this region. Believe me we need America as much as you need her, for the prosperity of the poor world. There are many ways to defuse the problem but only one way to escalate it by continuing the existing policy. I can assure you Mr. President that there is great potential in Pakistan to help round of the situation. They have the will to make a way, you have to assist them to make it quickly. Doubting Pakistan intelligence agencies is indeed declaring no confidence in Pakistan government. Such intentions do not solve but complicate the matter. There is no other way but to help each other get out of the mess.

Middle East is another hotspot to melt. It is burning since 1948 and the west, especially the American establishment is apparently and continuously putting fuel to keep this fire alive. Mr.President you have to be an independent judge to pass the fair judgment. A partisan judgment by many of your ex presidents have not been accepted by the world. You don't have to be a special category judge but an ordinary real British or American judge to administer justice. By God we will beg Palestinians to abide by your judgment. Since Jews have also put their blood to develop this land I will personally suggest a South African arrangement and solution. A fair and acceptable solution will take care of at least 60 percent of world terrorism. A separate state of Israel and Palestine is merely a hoax and may never be transformed into reality. It will never be treated judicially by the west and therefore why indulge in deception and hypocrisy.

Iran's independent policy must be appreciated and respected. Any disagreement affecting the world community must be negotiated and discussed, (by the way world community does not only constitute America, Britain, France, Germany and Canada the rest of the world population also counts. Your community of 540 millions must respect the rest of the six billions also living side by side.

Iran has enough resources to exist without any help from world community; they have enough to eat, plenty of water to drink and the free air, a gift of nature to survive. The spirit of freedom that they have, can outlast them even if you bring them back to Stone Age, the maximum threat that Mr. Bush was hiding in his pockets. Believe me the modern world is immune to this kind of threat now. Let us all learn to live in peace and harmony.

In the UN Racist Conference at Geneva, from 12-14 April 09, Iranian President **Ahmadinejad** had the courage to speak against the atrocities of Israel on the Palestinians. The Americans who keep calling Iran as axis of evil and her European cronies who follow them in praise of Israel should have had the courage to listen to Mr. Ahmadinejad. If the rest of the world community had the patience to listen a few of you in favour of Israel, you should have also the courage to listen the truth also.

Lastly my prayers and appetite that I had wished in my paper of provoking a change: I—On 4th Dec. 08, that bringing the people together is to solve the problems of terrorism spreading from the last 50 to 60 years. Peace and progress comes by bringing people together instead of segregating them forcefully through stringent visit restrictions. America and other rich countries are considered heaven by poor countries. Everyone likes to go to heaven. Visit visas to travel or for that matter to work may be relaxed so that people can interact with each other for mutual benefit, and take advantage of each other's expertise to work for the common cause of human welfare. The people involved in 9/11 are still controversial. The truth still hangs either in the air—or our Tel-Aviv.

History shows that migration of population has helped in progress and development. Peace was affected temporarily but generally people settled down with mutual consent, tolerance and positive behavior amongst each other. It is the blessing of immigration that your good father came to America and you are now the President of USA. I'm sure your present position will benefit America more than many presidents who served before you.

Note:

My article provoking a change was forwarded by my son with his personal note to President Obama which was warmly reciprocated.

The copy of the letter is reproduced and attached for your review.

THE WHITE HOUSE

WASHINGTON

June 26, 2009

Dear Friend:

Thank you for your kind note and enclosure. Your thoughtful words join a chorus of millions of Americans who are eager to lead our Nation towards a brighter tomorrow.

Each day, I am inspired by the encouraging messages of hope and determination I have received from people across the country. With the magnitude of challenges we face, we will only overcome them if our imagination is joined to common purpose.

The future we leave to our children and grandchildren will be determined by our willingness to shoulder each other's burdens, take great risks, and move forward as one people and one Nation. With your help, we will build on what we have already achieved and lay a foundation for real and lasting progress.

Sincerely,

In the Defence of Armed Forces

16ᵗʰ July 2009

Armed forces in Pakistan have an undisputed respect for them in every corner of the country. No one has to substantiate for them the immortal role they have played for their country. Their sacrifices from 1947 till to date have enough proof to honour their loyalty and place them at the highest standing in the country. The performance in Kashmir, Rann of Kutch, 1965 can be graded as a feat of highest degree of patriotism. The only set back they suffered was the battle of 1971 which everyone knows was due to their own stupid and poor civilian leadership who went for their personal gains rather than the country. The Chief of Army Staff at times exploited or capitalized the power of the armed forces and misused its obedience to discipline for their own advantage and took over the country as dictators whenever they found any unrest or an apparent danger to Pakistan. There were indeed such conditions existing which rightly or wrongly warranted some kind of safety to stabilize the country, especially in the wake of strong enemy trying to destroy Pakistan.

Pakistan armed forces had the distinction to perform so bravely against five times bigger enemy in all the wars. In 1947, in spite of being totally under equipped they gifted Azad Kashmir to Pakistan and forced India to go to UNO to prevent their onslaught by accepting Kashmir; a disputed territory. In 1965 the army defeated India in almost all four fronts and Pakistan Air-force broke the old myth of battle of Britain, and the whole world recognized the superiority of PAF over their three times numerically superior and better equipped with modern air craft. Pakistan Navy kept the entire Indian Navy tied at their dockyards throughout the war. 1971 marred their earlier achievements because of their poor army leadership and political leaders' duplicity and treachery.

14ᵗʰ Aug'1947 to 1957 there were seven Prime Ministers, some for a few years, a few for a few months and yet one for a few days. Mr. Nehru had the audacity to say that Pakistan was changing Prime Ministers more frequently than he changed his shirts. Skindar Mirza who was part of the civil government ultimately got fed up and invited Gen. Ayub Khan to impose martial law to stabilize the country. Ayub Khan realising that responsibility without authority would be a serious reprimand on him, got rid of Sikandar Mirza and took over the country as the first martial law administrator. It was though a very bad precedence but in the wake of democracy on the death bed, there was no choice but to stabilize the country to face external and internal threats. He was supported by most of the civilian political leaders to develop the country economically and militarily. Disregarding the prejudice so deeply entrenched in the minds of our civilian leadership against the armed forces, a neutral observer would find Ayub Khan's era as a golden period of our history and so was acclaimed throughout the world, especially in Asia and Middle East. The industrialization and educational reforms, the green revolution in agriculture were the world's best standpoint of that time; so much so that our entire five years plan was high jacked by South Korea to transform their country as an Asian Tiger.

There were of course many failings and comings because God Almighty was not himself running this country, He had assigned this responsibility on a few human beings, and we all know that, "to err is human". Even democracy has such imperfections.

A few intellectuals regard Ayub Khan as the prime source of sowing the seeds of separation between East and West Pakistan. Without going too much into the history, to them I can only quote a few things which might persuade them that for God's sake, 'hath holla rakho'. The first jute mill, the biggest in Asia at that time, was established in his time. Then a few textile mills to utilize the raw material from West Pakistan. The grant for inter marriages special allowances for East and West Pakistani personnel was provided as honorarium to bring them closer to each other. He also arranged migration of poor agriculture families in large scale from East Pakistan and provided free land, live stocks, houses, plus mobilization funds to settle down in West Pakistan.

The purpose is not to compliment the martial law but to express a few details and facts before the public to know and understand the difference instead of polluting their minds with the prejudiced propaganda. Martial law indeed was a bad experience but not as bad as our civilian leaders have done to this poor country. **It would therefore be fair to analys, "kia khoya, kia paya", of the entire stretch of that time.**

As for West Pakistan; besides substantial industrialization, Tarbaila Dam, the biggest earthen dam in the world, Mangla Dam, and many other small projects for agriculture developments were the spectacles of Ayub Khan's planning. The buying of Gwadar and adjoining area from Ameer of Qatar, showed the foresight of this soldier statesman, the golden project that today every civilian talks about and takes advantage, was the vision of Ayub Khan's government.

Ayub Khan had many serious faults which cannot be condoned. He must be blamed for his bad deeds but for God's sake don't deprive him for the good things and directions he provided for which Pakistan is still getting the fruits of.

Yahya Khan was a stupid General like many other generals and civilian leaders who damaged their countries. They are therefore remembered in the same manner. However, I just want to put the record straight, when he held the elections, all civilian politicians without any exceptions and intellectuals were paying big tribute to him for this act of fairness and piety. You may take out the newspapers of that time to see for yourselves. He should have been punished for his bad deeds but was saved because a few civilian leaders' heads would also be rolled.

The political prophet and the darling of our people of that time, Mr. Zulfiqar Ali Bhutto, should also be placed on record for the people to judge his conduct as a ruler. The following few points maybe a reminder to those who have forgotten the intricacies of the national politics of his policies.

i.   Intentionally ill advised Yahya Khan on Army action and misbehaved at Security Council debate (by tearing off the Polish resolution), which could have served as face saving for Pakistan from the humiliation of defeat and new relationship with East Pakistan. This was purposely done to ensure his take over in West Pakistan.

ii. Destroyed national discipline by inciting undesirable elements to ruin the economic Base of the country by humiliating industrialists and investors by their workers.

iii. Nationalizing and damaging all industry and even the educational institutions down from Matric level schools. Gen. Zia ul Haq and Benazir had to reverse the process of nationalization and denationalized all the prominent progressive institutions.

iv. The only good thing was calling Islamic Summit at Lahore and set the ball rolling on nuclear track. This was a huge political credit for him.

v. During first election in 1977 introducing rigging by government machinery and creating anarchy in the country where army refused to fire at their own people.

vi. He was forced to negotiate a compromise with PNA but immediately set out on foreign trip thereby delaying the implementation of the agreement which encouraged Army to intervene and takeover.

vii. Kidnapping member of opposition from Larkana to brag about unopposed election for himself. He was also famous for setting up Dalai camp for punishing his own party rebel members and disgracing J. Rahim, the party Sectary General by the ghonda element of his party.

Air Marshal Asghar Khan, a failed political soldier who turned down Mr. Bhutto's proposal for making fool of the poor masses of the country and rule them as his partner. His unsuccessful political career still is full of respect by all segment of society even today. His failure in politics is no loss to him as a person but loss to the nation for not having an honest and clean politician.

Gen. Zia ul Haq, the most ineligible out of all the Generals, unfortunately took over as the third dictator in the country. His regime was full of turmoil but the least corrupt amongst all the rulers since 1958. In spite of all the flaws, he had the courage to look into the eyes of our enemy, India, and created conditions which warranted them to bother about their own security more than creating problems for Pakistan. The Sikh problem and insurgency in Kashmir kept their eyes away from Pakistan as long as Zia ul Haq was in command.

Mr. Bhutto's execution was the biggest allegation on Zia ul Haq and apparently this charge could not be cleared during his lifetime and after.

During Russian invasion of Afghanistan he dealt with Americans better than any civilian leader would have done. His policies defeated Soviets and forced their retreat back to Russia. With Soviet Union disintegrated, many small Muslim states emerged out of it thereby providing better chances of trade and relations for futuristic links with Pakistan. It is another matter that none of the civilians or military leaders of Pakistan had the sense of taking any advantage out of it.

After Zia ul Haq's crash, Gen. Mirza Aslam Baig had a unique opportunity to take over the country but he voluntarily opted to stay away and requested President Ishaq to arrange a civilian change to take over as per the constitution. This was the commendable vision of Gen. Aslam Beig for which the armed forces were awarded Tamgha e Jumhuriat by the next Prime Minister, Benazir Bhutto.

The point of significance is that no General wants to involve himself in government affairs if the conditions are normal and there is no turmoil in the country. Gen. Aslam Baig must be given credit for not meddling with power without purpose and voluntarily staying away from it.

Benaiz was the next Prime Minister of the country, whose first sermon to the PPP stalwarts was "Paisay banao kyon kay aagay election larna hai". As a result people like Faisal Saleh Hayatt, Sher Pao,and other adventurers were all out to loot the country. Her latest find was Mr. Zardari, who followed her advice meticulously and acquired a famous award of Mr. 10%. When it became really unbearable, she was dismissed by her own president, Mr. Farooq Leghari to put an end to her misdeeds.

Benazir made sure to bail out India from the instability of Khalistan by handing over the list of all Sikh leaders through one of her most trusted leaders. Even removed Kashmir's name from the road signs in Islamabad to reassure Rajiv Gandhi that Kashmir was no problem between India and Pakistan. Her coming back from exile with NRO blessing was indeed to provide support to Musharaf for continuing as the president and her as his prime minister. What happened subsequently is all a story and description.

Then came Nawaz Sharif, known to be politically naive and no match to Benazir by the PPP leaders. However, as an average man, I personally think he did the best after Prime Minister Liaqat Ali Khan. His plans of Motor ways, communication, free movement of foreign exchange, privitization of some government assets, NFC award, water distribution to provinces, and above all the nuclear detonation, against the will of super power and other Western countries, goes to his credit and credit for the country.

Gen. Musharaf was next to follow as the worst of Military dictators we had. His coward actions, misguided and short sighted policies have done maximum damage to Pakistan. Only God knows how long will it take for Pakistan to recover from this remorse.

The present civilian leadership is as irrelevant as was Musharaf. People now have fairly good judgement about their performance. In one and a half years the promises they broke, the useless visits abroad and impotence they have shown in running the country is a disgrace. Their predecessors were very keen to re-elect Gen. Musharaf in uniform. I hope the present regime does not follow the same course and recall him to guide them and teach them the good governance for the five years of their elected period.

Military dictatorship was a curse and hopefully we never face it anymore. Civilian incompetency and corrupt leadership was a bigger curse and we pray to Allah that we never have such leaders anymore ruling this country. Let us forget the past and drive onto the civil road map efficiently to put the dictatorship at our back, never to return. However, the saying: worst democracy is better than the best dictatorship is not a Quranic verse but a Western gimmick to derail countries like China and Pakistan. Democracy established in Afghanistan and Iraq by the

West may be an eye opener for us all. Every country has their own political conditions to suite them and in this modern world everyone should 'mind his own business', and let the freedom of will by their own people prevail.

The Wicked War

9th September 2009

War is a game with no probable draw. Everyone is a loser and of course there is no winner. Afghanistan war is nothing but destruction. All sides seem fed up but no one accepts his mistake or guilt committed. Eight long years have not taught them any lesson. Many lives have been lost, people are in distress, mothers and children are crying, yet their leaders are insisting to go beyond a draw. People are suffering, loss of jobs, America and England in grave recession, their banks are falling apart and the business is drowning. The world economic system has almost crumbled. The people of Afghanistan have nothing else except precious lives to lose for the last twenty-five to thirty years. They are left only with foreign troops and a possible light at the end of the tunnel.

I was fed up of listening and reading about the killing of hundreds everyday and witnessing coffins of my officers and soldiers coming from tribal areas of Pakistan. I decided to runaway to seek peace, harmony, and calmness for a few days. I have an inborn affinity with London, and decided to avail a break to get away from sadness and heartaches. After a few days of relief I started witnessing the same traumatics of coffins of British soldiers from Afghanistan rolling out of the Military aircraft's tail. It is almost a daily affair since I have come to London. The same pathetic scenes because of which I had run away from Pakistan, where I saw many such coffins of my sons like officers and soldiers coming from Afghan-Pakistan border and being buried by their relations. I could feel the depth of their grief, while they were speaking of being proud of their deeds in service of their country. Exactly in the same manner, the English parents were giving interviews of the loss of their children and the wives of their husbands. Their small children totally feeling-less of what had happened and completely unaware of their future, were looking bewildered to see their fathers lying in coffin whom they had bade farewell a little while ago. It was the same pain and frustration in London as was in Pakistan. The same emotional speeches from the leaders about the sacrifices they had done for the country and cause.

Mr. Bush led Tony Blair to Afghanistan to fight Al Qaeda because of 9/11. Then they involved all the NATO countries for the same purpose. Pakistan was forced under duress to join the war, basically to be a party and cushion for future escalation. No one from all these leaders questioned about the alternative available to avoid the catastrophe of such attack on a small group of people and the poorest country of the world. This could have probably been done with a mere threat, to discuss on the table. After fighting so many unsuccessful wars they have not yet learnt something more rational and appropriate to sort out the mutual differences. The war in Afghanistan has now transformed from personal vengeance into a global conflict. For America and the West, it appears to be a matter of prestige where as it is a life or death for Pakistan.

9/11 was basically an instigating factor to attack Afghanistan. Taking irrational action in haste and that also by the powerful is conceivable but continuation of the folly is totally incomprehensible. Osama Bin Laden under protection by the Taliban government was considered responsible for the attack on Twin Towers; however, the cause of this action could have been perceived later to put an end to such incidents in future. All characters allegedly involved were Arabs and they must have a strong cause to commit this insanity against a super power with nuclear capability of unlimited strength, capable of destroying small and big sized targets, at will. It had to be a desperate moment for them, "to be or not to be", to commit this crime.

The cause is known to every proclaimed authority and the people but unfortunately they behave hypocritical when it comes to facing the truth. They go round and round without stopping at a confirmed moral rendezvous. They are more worried to protect their neutrality than to stand by the truth. They are the real culprits of this so called global village, where every neighbour protects only the other neighbour of wealth and authority. No one talks of poor Palestinians, the majority of whom are living as outcasts outside their own country, and those living in their own country are no better than the untouchables. 9/11 might have been the stunt of Palestinians or their Arab associates but it was definitely because of this unfortunate country occupied illegally by Jews, exported by the West from Europe to establish a country of Israel. The reality is for the history to dig out the truth about the 9/11.

After World War II Hitler was punished and Germany destroyed. Holocaust was one of the reasons for all the debris shifted to Palestine. However, if it was paramount to do so, there must have been some safeguards and adjustments made between the natives and the imported elements. That very debris has now come up as beautiful buildings, shopping plazas, dwelling palaces, and fascinating cities in Palestine. The unfortunate part is the original owners shunted out to inhabit tent cities in the neighbouring countries or shoved in the different corners of their own country. Hopefully one day there is some realization by the new settlers to accept the real owners to come and live together to cherish mutual peace and tranquillity. Have separate worship places but enjoy happiness together, otherwise these very debris maybe heading back one day as a fate accompli of the history. The Jews contribution of this area is recognized beyond doubt but for this you cannot destroy the country and establish new units. Both the communities should be absorbed in a way to keep the original identity of the country and the entire population including Jews to form a democratic entity and exist like blacks and whites in South Africa. This would create harmony and affinity rather than everlasting feud and enmity. Defacing Palestine is the cause which created the 9/11.

Afghanistan war is becoming very serious. It is no more a war with Al Qaeda or Osama Bin Laden; it is a war between the people of Afghanistan and America, England, and NATO. You may call them Taliban or the Tribals of Pakistan-Afghan border origin, they are the same kind of people and have been living and fighting as friends and brothers against out-siders. I hope after these eight long years of war, the West has viewed the future strategy to end this calamity. "To talk or rot is the only option". Talking indeed is the only recipe. The British commanders have complained about the quality of weapons and equipment. I wonder if that would help in any turnround. Taliban have no compatible weapons to fight nor do they have any factories to develop them. They only have the spirit and that I am afraid is picking up more momentum with the passage of time.

The plan to shift the war to Pakistan has not succeeded. However, for a few weeks there was quite a bit of respite in Afghanistan while Pakistan was burning. The author of this strategy thought that they had hit the bull's eye but Pakistan proved stronger than was expected. Its forces showed their metal to subside the so called revolt arranged by the friends of Pakistan. However, they still need some time to control the situation fully.

I feel some civilian elements in Pakistan still hold a motivating influence and have the capacity to steer Taliban leadership in Afghanistan to focus on a peaceful path which will not embarrass the allies nor cause humiliation to the Taliban and other Afghans. Government of Pakistan is unable to play a part in this task because they had already burnt their boats by joining the janta. The janta still has a chance to change, if only they stop acting like a godfather in the case. The civilian elements maybe solicited to help stop this small conflict growing into a big war.

The World War I and II lasted for almost nine years with millions of causalities. The Afghan war in 9th year is a matter of serious concern for all concerned. 9/11 seems to be a forgotten story now. It has now changed and become a war of women liberation and democracy. Irrespective of Karzai brand democracy or any other trade mark, no name is good enough to justify the continuation of this senseless war. The American commanders have spoken; the British commanders have endorsed the same, Pakistan is crying to wrap up. Majority of American and British people are in favour of its termination. The leaders have to wake up to the call of their people. Let them not behave like American leaders who always told their people that losing Vietnam would be losing the entire South East Asia. That was a lie, and today the apprehension of the leaders that the safety of United States and West lies in fighting the terrorism in Afghanistan is vague and a bigger lie.

This wicked war in Afghanistan must stop otherwise I personally feel that there is no shelter to avoid seeing such miseries anywhere in the world. I decided to return to Pakistan and stand by my own people to share their grief and make efforts to end this wicked war to provide relief to our brothers and sisters in England and America to receive happy soldiers coming back, to share their joys, not the coffins to increase their pain.

European Union Role model for Indo-Pak Subcontinent

15th September 2009

I happened to attend an event at Nehru Centre London, on 3rd Sept'09. I was lucky to meet lots of well wishers of both India and Pakistan. It was basically a goodwill social function to promote Asghar Wajahat's play 'Jis Lahore Nai Dehkya O Jamyai Nai'. Almost all speakers were repentant of the Indian Partition and loss of human lives on both sides. It was such a cordial atmosphere that most of the outsiders thought both countries' were about to declare a European like Union very soon. However, I observed a few unhappy pessimist faces who were heard discussing it as a mission impossible.

I personally felt very fine sentiments expressed by some of the speakers. It was surprising to learn that most of them were very hardliner Indians. At the outset I was very impressed and thanked some of them for their fine feelings for Pakistan. I had very frank discussions with one of the visitors without exchanging any introduction. He was reluctant to disclose his identity and I thought it appropriate not to insist and both of us remained strangers for quite some time. He suddenly asked me to call him 'Chandar' and I reciprocated with 'Choudhry'. He never offered any visiting card and I kept mine in the pocket. I guessed he was a politician belonging to the sitting Indian government because this function was basically organized by an Indian association and I was there due courtesy of an Indian girl studying with my daughter.

During the very informal discussion, I told him that Mr. Jinnah was very bold and frank with the Indian Leadership, Mr. Gandhi, Nehru, and Patel, to avoid the partition in lieu of special status and security for Muslim community's rights as equal citizens in the undivided India. This was virtually declined by the two at the 1946 Cabinet Mission held under Lord Pethick Lawrence, the Secretary of State for India. This has also been published in the recent book Jinnah: India-Partition-Independence, in which Mr. Jaswant Singh praising Mr. Jinnah and accusing Mr.Nehru and Patel for this act of dividing "Bharat Mata into two". Mrs. Indra Gandhi made it three in 1971, and felt very proud of it. The prejudice is still so strong that poor Jaswant Singh is not able to sell his books in some of the States' in India. However, this bias has been neutralized and has become a source of advertisement for the book. Mind you Jaswant Singh was no friend of Pakistan when he was the Foreign Minister in BJP Government. He was then a political leader but has now come down to earth and realized that the truth must be told to people as history's property and asset.

Chandar was very kind and patient to listen to my criticism undisturbed. However, he asked me point-blank, if I was in politics. He felt a sigh of relief that I was a retired Air force officer who fought all the wars with India. I was in Air Defence and had the privilege to control and got the first Indian Canberra Spy Plane shot down in 1959 near Rawalpindi and also the last Indian Raider Mig 21 on the last day of 1971 war, near Pasroor in West Pakistan.

At this stage I thought Chandar was definitely a diplomat, otherwise he would have objected to my narration of the war incidents. I was glad to be talking to a real down to earth gentleman. He put his hand on my shoulder and argued for reconciliation and forget-and-forgive approach. Frankly as a soldier I was getting a little apprehensive about his good behaviour and wanted to round off the conversation as meaningless by both on account of lack of any authority and connection with the governments to have any contribution for the cause. He probably sensed my feeling and told me that he had a good business in London, his father had migrated to England in 1950's but he thought there were more chances for us all and for our coming generations in Indo-Pak Subcontinent if some kind of accord takes place between India and Pakistan. He said this was his passion as an Indian today and his roots in Pakistan before partition.

Irrespective of whether we both could help reduce tension or bring some reconciliation, 90% of the people gathered there craved for peace between the two countries. I provoked him with a wish if this kind of spirit existed with Hindu Leadership of that time; there wouldn't be a Pakistan today. However, I was very frank in telling him that the present change I feel is because Pakistan is a physical reality now and as strong militarily as India. All these sympathies and concessions are being showered because of this. To return to brotherhood fold and new relationship like European Union of course is for the benefit of both the countries. India is a big brother and like traditional honour of this title in the Subcontinent, India must offer some generosity to come to terms on core issues like Kashmir, rest of the small problems will automatically settle with passage of time. There is no way to get closer without solving Kashmir in accordance with the wishes of its people and both India and Pakistan agreeing to their wishes. The rut of 'Attott Ang' has to be buried as it was accepted a disputed territory by Mr. Nehru and the UNO in 1948. One day kashmiris have to get the right of self determination, why not today? This will demonstrate a natural pull towards each other. I am sure this may form the basis to start a communion like European Union.

Indian and Pakistani troops are facing each other all along the borders. Small instances at times are unavoidable particularly when the relationship is not good and tempers are high. However, It does not warrant to stop talking and create war-like situation, especially by the big brother. Kargil was a senseless operation started by Gen. Musharaf but at the end of the day, went to India's way. Humiliation in the world was enough punishment for Pakistan. Any more than that would have destroyed half of India and Pakistan. Such happening should not deter us to take our eyes off from the main aim. Mr. Vajpayee stopped talking to Nawaz Sharif, even after knowing the real story. Similarly Bombay attack by some extremists was another stupidity which brought both the countries at the brink of war, and it has taken us almost one year to talk to each other again. Similar type of incident where a very serious bombing attack at Grand Hotel Brighton was done on 12th Oct 1984 where PM Margaret Thatcher, government Ministers, and Conservative Party members were staying for a conference. IRA terrorists carried out attack at 02:00hrs in the morning, which were so intense that PM's bathroom was damaged. Besides other casualties, one MP and a Minister's wife were killed. This attack was no less than the Taj Mahal Hotel Bombay, but Mrs. Thatcher addressed the conference at 09:00hrs the same day as scheduled to show how little importance was given to IRA terrorists. That is how mature leaders of mature nations behave in crisis. They kept talking to IRA and today most of their differences have been settled.

We are almost one and a half billion people living in the subcontinent with different diversity, religion, and culture. One should not expect all hunky-dory at all times, especially so when innumerable issues are unsettled and need solution. The main aim of promoting good will and good relationship must be kept in sight always. Unfortunately personal interest of politicians is always a big hindrance in the way of peace and people do not understand the evil behind these usual patriotism gossips of these leaders.

We both need strong leaders who are capable of taking unpopular decisions to solve the problems of our two nations. India being the big brother has more responsibility in this connection. Mr. Vajpayee was the right man to do it, but unfortunately I feel he was guided onto the wrong track on more than one occasions. The present PM Manmohan Singh is too weak and meek to take any daring decision and so is Sonia Gandhi. The reason is known to everyone and needs no further explanation. Mr. Manmohan Singh behaves apologetic talking, with one eye on congress and the other on Pakistan. I wish he behaves like a traditional Sikh as known to us all in the Subcontinent.

I feel Pakistan has been very open and has come a long way to start afresh with India. Hyderabad and Juna-garh States are a forgotten claim, East Pakistan loss, an ignored story, what more is expected out of a small neighbour? I am sure the Indian leadership must have learnt the lesson from history. Jaswant Singh has shown them the mirror after a long time. They may not turn their faces to the other side. Let them skin-off the prejudice and refrain from the exercise . . . .

'Hamiasha dair kar deta hun mein'

(I am always late in taking action)

The Black President

Barack Hussein Obama was destined to reach the place nature had decided to fix up for him. He understands the white itch but he is acting like every good leader endeavors to protect his country and people against such foul gossips. He knew all poor, white and blacks, Asians and Hispanics, wanted a change for themselves. They had been exploited for a long time specifically for the last eight years of Bush and Party. The riches and even the upper middle class of Whites have been trying hard to stop this history's turn about and prejudice that a few brought from their ancestors and teachings of their parents about the superiority of colour which God had bestowed upon them as a matter of their birth rights.

I don't understand how God would create disparity amongst his creation without reason and bring prejudice between his own sons and daughters because of colour. The President's hypothesis settled on the option between good and bad in moral values, not on material acquisitions through illegitimate practices. Accomplishments on account of struggle and honest hard work for the life achievements are dear to him. However, to run his kingdom he has to designate some as leaders and the others subordinates to keep cohesion, discipline, and order for their own good and pleasant living and behaviour amongst each other.

The groups, clans, countries, and regions were conferred on the people according to the environments and a reasonable span of control. A sudden population explosion deprived some with loss of education, development, and advancement, which unfortunately brought dominance of one group or the country of position over the others. Some races to dominate the others. The Greeks, Romans, Persians, Arabs, and Mongols over others and at times Whites over Blacks and Brown. These changes kept happening at different intervals so that the rulers keep peace and calm in the world. This was test of their ability and potential to govern their subjects. The moment rulers misbehaved and exceeded their power, and subjects their tolerance limits, there was invariably a change to follow. This principle has generally been exercised by nature, and God only knows how long it will take to reach its climax or finality. The one in command unfortunately always tries to keep the status quo forever without keeping in mind the power of nature to set in motion the new changes.

Obama maybe symbol of the same process and change. Whites of America should be happy of this change coming out of the same country. Their dominance still remains in the world and it would be better for the agencies not to interfere in the Nature's scheme of working unless Obama himself defaults, or the poor people who brought him through God's will get fed-up of his performance. They must acknowledge the quiet sound waves which knocked at the Nature's door to bring the change, who knows how many tears were counted to remodel the whole setup and reconstruct the new world.

He is a bright man working apparently for those who brought him in the White House. The poor and have-nots seem to be happy and satisfied so far with his performance. His domestic policies appear to bring up the downtrodden in line with the upper class and their children with equitable education and treatment. It is natural that the upper class is feeling threatened with the fear of being deprived of their share and place in society, but are actually misguided with their wrong convictions. It, in fact should bring pleasure and happiness to see smiling faces around, rather miserable gloomy ones watching to take away something from them.

America is a God gifted country with tremendous resources to look after its own population along with the people of other poor countries. That would be their contribution to compensate the blessing of nature bestowed upon them.

The present world is full of discriminations and injustices by strong against the weak and usurpers against the destitute. It is no more a global village in the real sense as comprehended and envisaged by our forefathers. The community no longer looks after the neighbors but keeps on looking for a chance to pounce and take away whatever they possess. The problems of Palestine, Kashmir, Afghanistan, Iraq, and maybe Iran remind us to move quickly and save this good earth from getting disintegrated.

Palestine problem is within a jumps' reach if United States and the West want to solve it fairly. If South Africa with miles of differences between Whites and Blacks, with centuries disparities resolved to peaceful living amongst each other, why can't Israelis and Palestinians live together with a very little difference in their way of living and approach. Mr. Obama has to preach fairness and justice to West and Israeli's to come down to a reasonable decree. Jew's firm grip over the world economy is welcomed but maybe shared to multiply not to incapacitate the nations under their financial control. Where will they take their assets if they are not accepted by the leading countries and poor consumers. Destruction of world economy is not in favour of these masters themselves.

Kashmir is a nuclear flashpoint between Pakistan and India that can create massive destruction which the world has not so far seen since its creation. Mr. Richard Holbrook's thinking that Afghanistan is the problem of all the neighboring and Western countries but Kashmir is a problem only between India and Pakistan couldn't be more painful and selfish by one of the important leaders of the world today. His indifference can bring the biggest catastrophe in the world. It is realized as a grave but simple problem by the majority of people of India and Pakistan, yet they need somebody to mediate and show the way acceptable to both. There is no better country than USA and President Obama to put this problem on a judicious route today.

Afghanistan was the creation of Mr. Bush, the then president of America and is incumbent on Obama to bring it to the end. Al Qaeda might have been the cause but due to American folly have been subsequently mixed up with Taliban. Pakistan was trapped under duress and suffered no less than Afghanistan. America was the cause of it, however, the people of America and England are fed-up of the war and everybody is looking up to Obama to take it to its culmination.

Iraq has been destroyed by America and England for no reasons other than Israel. Iraq was the only possible Arab country to upset the future plan of the West. It was therefore decided to fabricate fake weapons of mass destruction, an excuse to disintegrate her and incapacitate her to face Israel for all times to come. The West failed to do this, but was successful in the ultimate for the time being. However, I am sorry it brought the maximum insult afflicted on America in terms of shoes thrown on the face of her president. Mr. Obama may vindicate that damage done to this great country, USA, in his own convenience.

Iran presents no threat to Arabs, nor Arabs create any problem for Iran, and so is the case with Europe and America. They are only worried about Israel's safety and they think Iran stands a threat to her because of Ahmedinejad's convictions. With Palestinian problem solved, the Iranian dilemma will automatically subside provided America is willing to create new relationship. Sanctions against Iran will destroy her coming generation. China with a very high moral value and Russia as a member of the Asian community should refrain to be a part to this destruction.

I personally like Obama, the black president. And feel very strongly that he has been brought from the most backward country to the most blessed country to achieve the biggest award and honour for this nation to resurrect the falling world to a new start to prove that the nature has the power to take work from someone, people least expecting to materialize. Allow me to congratulate the poor people of United States who accepted nature's call to elect a black man as a change, on the call of nature.

This is my itch!

Beware of Afghan War Sequel

1ˢᵗ December 2009

There was a time in 19th century when sun never set in British Empire. One of the regions included Afghanistan and the tribal zone located between Afghanistan and Pakistan of today. The British ruled it (if it was called a rule) for almost eighty years. Their forces were restricted to fortress at night and had off and on rounds of civil streets to show their presence and demonstrate lawful control of the country. The enforcement of law was also practiced by the courts inside the fortress of the armed forces. They ultimately retreated to North West Frontier Province (NWFP) of Indian union with unforgettable memories of sufferings in terms of army and civilian casualties. Let me remind my readers in the UK and NATO countries about those horrible stories including William Brydon's return to NWFP with one man out of sixteen thousand and five hundred troops.

I think the British are masters in knowledge of this area and they must honestly embark upon disseminating the same to the Americans and other new occupants about the consequences and what future holds for them in the long run. This may help them to decide to leave now or after ten years or more. The American and British Generals have been honest and out spoken in expressing their opinion to their governments but their governments have their own political aims and resolves. They are probably influenced by the corrupt Afghan leadership or the agencies including media reps and think-tank's assessments in those environments. These intellectuals have their own focus and designs especially when they are directed to adopt a line of action, to either confuse the issue or betray the people. They fabricate plans and draw the conclusions as directed. This is the reason why adventures in Iraq and Afghanistan keep extending like a magic rope and ultimately explode to no one's advantage. The suffering in terms of innocent lives and economic deprivation are forgotten as a past history without any accountability.

Attacking Afghanistan in October'2001 in search of a small group of Al Qaeda was a big folly and forcing Pakistan into the war was a bigger one. Pakistan could have been a main neutralizing factor to each of the situation with diplomatic offensive and threat warning to Talibans. Unfortunately they adopted the last option which was a grave miscalculation and was ultimately bound to fail. Afghanistan of course has suffered a great deal; Pakistan has undergone a big turmoil with loss of lives, economic collapse and destabilisation of its borders and internal security. America has suffered economic disaster due to war spending in Afghanistan and Iraq. The NATO members and other allies are fed up to chip in for the war machinery instead of providing social and economic aid to the affected countries to stand on their own feet.

Pakistan was forcibly escorted to this war by Mr. Bush. Since then we have had not a day of peaceful living. Besides about two thousand regular army troops, we have lost about ten thousand civilians of both the friendly and opposing citizens at all fronts. After all those misdirected elements fighting with our troops are also people of our own origin and their loss is also our loss. Pakistan had a rising economy in 21st century and with freedom of East Asians Muslim states from Soviet Union, we had the opportunity of becoming one of the most affluent nations in the near future. Becoming part of this war has pushed us backwards for at least fifty years if not more. Due to the unrest and instability, industry cannot take its root and thrive. Increase in suicidal attacks at tourist resorts has completely finished this industry. People are living in an environment of fear. A few attacks on educational institutes have had horrendous effect and parents keep praying for the safe return of their children from schools and educational institutes. Business is suffering because people are scared of visiting the markets. Exports are dwindling because businessmen are not sure and hence shy of investing and promoting the business. No international team is ready to play in Pakistan for lack of security and terrorism. Slowly and slowly Pakistan is moving down towards deficit in every sphere and heading in the direction of a failed state.

Afghan war is creating misunderstanding and tension between India and Pakistan whether it is with or without the consent of our American and British friends. India thinks her dream and desire of breaking Pakistan is being realized. Frankly speaking Mr. Manmohan Singh's recent respect in the White House (with a small natural jealousy) would have been shared as respect of the whole people of the subcontinent. But his conspiracy with Obama and Netanyahu against Pakistan is intolerable. Indian activities in Afghanistan, her ventures in Baluchistan, and her unreasonable manoeuvring in Kashmir are seen as a grave concern in Pakistan. American and British rhetoric that this matter is only between India and Pakistan is as absurd as Afghanistan and Al Qaeda is a matter between Afghanistan and America only. You cannot use Pakistan for your purpose and become unmindful of her life and death problems. Everything that is vital for Pakistan's existence is affecting the war in Afghanistan. You cannot force 'do more' philosophy in Afghanistan while encouraging stab in the back policy in Kashmir. War is more a state of mind to win or lose irrespective of the possession of modern and lethal weapons. Pakistan's concern about Kashmir must be addressed judicially to restore confidence between Pakistan and her allies in war.

We in Pakistan are quite mindful of Indian dreams in Afghanistan. India should realize that we also have some dreams. The Muslims had ruled India for over a thousand years. We are both nuclear states now. We all pray that we are not led to a stage to use these weapons against each other and encourage Afghanistan to see new dream of the history repeating itself in this region.

Mr. Brown has suddenly become active against Taliban and Al Qaeda. Maybe it is his new dream in the wake of coming election in the UK. However, violence begets violence and is not to be promoted in any form. He is very important partner in Afghanistan and should hold patience instead of provoking negative pursuit. Tony Blair joined Bush and landed in this mess, and Mr. Brown should not follow the same trail. 'DO MORE' philosophy must change its course towards peaceful direction and not towards drone attacks for killing innocent women and children with an excuse to find one odd undesirable character. How long can you continue with this satanic approach to kill people. People are the asset and they must be preserved and talked to end this disaster. Let us not repeat Moscow's destruction after Napoleon's attack and Hitler's army's aftermath in Leningrad in World War II.

Every New Year traditionally brings hope for better prospects for the people. Unfortunately more suffering is coming for the last nine years and that also from the most civilized and affluent people towards the extremely poor and deprived. We pray that the year 2010 may have the blessings from Mr. Barack Hussein Obama and Mr. Gordon Brown, for a gift of peace in Afghanistan and Pakistan. That is the only way to celebrate the coming New Year. We have had mourning for a long time. And indeed deserve a break now. The people had already given their verdict through demonstrations in London, Washington, and other capitals of the world but unfortunately the rulers had their own preference. Let them now join the people for this New Year.

Pakistan is the key to resolve Afghanistan crisis with or without Al Qaeda's input. Going too far in their war with Tribals may hamper the outcome for good. Peace comes with dialogue and negotiation and not by force. All reasonable people are hinting to stop this war. A little while ago Mr. Mathew Hoh, an American diplomat in Afghanistan, Maj. Gen. Andrew Mackay of UK, and now a German Chief of Army Staff has resigned against the continuous Afghan war. People of Pakistan, UK, and USA are crying hard to end this catastrophe. Let Obama and Brown join their heads to use reason and anticipate the Afghan war sequel \and let the people of this area live in peace and harmony.

The man under pressure in the White House

27ᵗʰ Jan 2010

Barack Hussein Obama created history during the last presidential elections and so did America and it's people to prove their commitment and obligations towards democracy. Irrespective of race, colour and creed all Whites, Blacks, Hispanics, and Asians stood by principles and merit to elect a well deserved Black candidate as their president, against the expectations of some prejudiced minority who tried their best to scandalize American conduct. The whole world however, saw the Americans coming out victorious in this test. Long live America and God bless the people of America.

Obama came with a mandate 'to change', the mentality of supremacy of the ruling Whites over others, and preserve human dignity and glory, from old courtiers who were averse to that change. His confirmation and strong endorsement of "yes we can" shook this old leadership to check and halt this trend of equality between masters and slaves and maintain the reflections of old traditions. The way things are being manoeuvred in the White House shows the beginning of weakening Obama's grip on the change, especially in the Middle East and Afghanistan. It reminds me about a novel, '**The Man**' by Irving Wallace that I read thirty-five years ago. It was a beautifully written fiction, which has now taken the shape of reality in the White House. It depicted a situation where an unexpected accident activated the law of succession that designated a black man Mr. Douglas Dilman as the first Black president of the United States of America. He had to bear the weight of his office, his race, and his private life. The man as president tried to uphold his oath in the face of international crisis, domestic dissensions, violence, scandals, and ferocious internal hostilities. The climax came when the senate met for the first time in hundred years to impeach the poor black president. The current circumstances seem to reflect the same fiction turning into reality in the White House today.

Obama's deliberations in the first few days in the White House gave an impression of freedom of actions where closure of Guantanamo Bay, retrieval of forces from Iraq, and reappraisal of Afghanistan war were the first on his agenda. Talking to Iran and North Korea was considered as part of the new policy. After one year in office, failure in all fields has proved that there were serious checks on the president to continue plans of his mandate. The change that he had perceived was put on hold presumably by the same forces, that were out to fail him in his mission. They could easily be identified by the people of vision.

Guantanamo Bay is still operative and no Federal State is ready to accept the transfer of so-called terrorists to their territory in spite of Commander in Chief's directive and intentions. This kind of defiance is not inadvertent but intentional and deliberate. One wonders why the president's mandate is being purposely shrugged off by most of the influential Whites and Jews around him. In fact there should have been an inquiry on Iraq War as initiated by the British; and the prisoners in Guantanamo Bay were exchanged with Mr. Bush and Tony Blair as war criminals.

The change in Afghan policy has fallen prey to the same old group who wanted to continue the operation with additional sixty thousand troops from America and NATO. In spite of four months strenuous efforts to bring a change, Mr. Obama failed to formulate a new Afghan policy to his liking and had to reconcile with a small shift by sending thirty thousand troops and culminate the operation within one and a half years. In real sense this seemed an escalation of war and unacceptable to the people of Afghanistan and I think the Tribals of Pakistan. Indian role in Afghanistan is further effecting the American-Pakistan relations and indeed the war in Afghanistan. I reiterate my submission written in one of previous paper that the solution lies in activating Pakistan's civilian elements to assist stopping this war. I sincerely feel that one woman ambassador like **Madeline Albright** can perform better and more effective than one division of Marines in the battle field.

Talking to Iran seems another letdown. Inflexible attitude on behest of Israel and American Jews is dramatizing the whole issue of Iranian nuclear episode. It is a doable project to restrict Iran from nuclear adventure through hard negotiation including other allied problems between Iran and America. No country in the world today could afford to stay away from America for her own future economic and other developments unless their integrity was hurt through threats of embargo and sanctions for no bonafide reasons. I personally think a broad based sanction against a country is a declaration of war against poor innocent children who ultimately suffer for lack of medicines and other nourishments for their growth. The children seldom forget such atrocities and disabilities as a result of such sanctions and that effects the long lasting relations between nations and countries.

Mr. President, Al-Qaeda maybe a menace but Israel is a curse. Both are to be tackled simultaneously to reach an equitable solution. Al Qaeda originated from the defenceless Palestinian blood, shed by the Israeli assassins through American tanks and F-16s. To eliminate Al-Qaeda the Israeli curse has to be transformed into some semblance of a decent change. Lopsided treatment would escalate into a bigger conflict as is evident from the current situation. Six million Israelis might as well realize that they are surrounded by three hundred million Arabs and Muslims. Time is not on their side. The sooner they come to terms with Palestinians the better it is for them. If twenty seven million Afghans are as fresh after fighting for eight years with a super power, Israel might face the same kind of situation for themselves in future. It is a matter of igniting a spark amongst the Arab ranks. The only durable solution is the South African model where both communities could live together and share the assets and resources of the country for their generations to come.

This is not the time for America to shut down embassies in Somalia and Yemen but open new avenues to address people's grievances otherwise you may have to wind up diplomatic relations with half of the world. The way America and the West is after Al-Qaeda and Taliban and deliberately taking no notice of Israel, unjustified wars with Iraq and Afghanistan, interference in Iran and occupation of Kashmir by India is driving the world towards Muslim/Christians or Muslim and non-Muslim divide which could be dangerous for the existence of the world itself. Countries like India, South Africa, Israel, Ethiopia, and Brazil, etc will again start playing the flute of neutrality like that of Marshal Tito, Col. Nasir, and Nehru to confuse the world with non-aligned movement in the Cold War era of 1950s. John Foster Dallas, the former Sectary of State, had rightly ascribed non-aligned and neutrality as immoral and short-sighted. The same concept might lead the present world to the same vicious circle to confuse the crucial disputes like Kashmir, Palestine, Iraq, and Afghanistan, unsolved and turning dangerous.

Obama partly owes his success to those who helped him achieve this remarkable position. People like Rahm Emanuel's family and other men of influence no doubt take credit for this and consider it their right to share authority in the White House. However, the poor people of America actually responsible for this fete, have bigger share in governance because the real power to elect Obama was the power of people not the tiny wealthy minority. The prayers of poor people around the earth had a special status that helped install Obama as the president of the United States. He should therefore realize his authority as a special agent of nature on earth. There is no doubt that he is sailing against vey strong headwinds but the power of constitution provide him the adequate strength to reach his destination and meet the promises made to the people of United States. Yielding on ordinary issues of minor consequence is understandable but compromising on vital issues like Iraq, Afghanistan and Palestine would be breaking the moral fibre of society. When it comes to principle you owe noting to no one and act like **Mosses** dealt with Pharaohs who brought him up in their own palaces.

Mr. Obama has no choice but to formulate new policies of equity and piety to lead the world as a sole leader of a single super power. I am sure the American people expect him to deliver in the same fashion. I hope he does not disappoint them and the millions of people around the world who prayed for his success.

Barack Hussein Obama took over as president on 20th Jan 2009. His first few days in the White House were very productive and indeed reflected the freedom of action from outside forces. Charged with the election spirit his priorities were stated in the following sequence:

1.) Closure of the Guantanamo Bay, which was the source of disgrace for American judiciary.

2.) Second option was to review the Afghan policy regarding already agreed sixty thousand additional troops. We all knew that he was reluctant to send any more troops. He resisted for almost four months but ultimately gave in for thirty thousand troops at the same time promising to wind up the operation within one and a half year.

3.) Terminate or conclude the mission in Iraq.

4.) Stop the policy of confrontation with Iran and resort to negotiations.

5.) To force Israel to establish the basis for a peaceful settlement.

Unfortunately all international commitments remain where they were before his takeover. The only credible achievement was healthcare reform bill for the poor American, which could not be set aside because of the internal pressure and very little opposition for political reasons.

We understand his compulsions but we expect him to face the adversaries with courage and superior intellect. Normal consultations and liberal process is the essence of democracy and majority decisions part of the system but we certainly would not appreciate a chosen representative of the poor people under arrest in the White House and being twisted by the prejudiced and obstinate old big-wigs. How he gets out of this pressure is a matter of time, and belief in the strength of nature, and commitment to the people. He must standby justice and fight the evil instead of compromise with it. That is the only way to transform the earth into heaven for all human beings.

In the Defence of General Zia-ul-Haq

5th April 2010

The constitution committee has recommended that Gen. Zia ul Haq be stripped off the honour of being the ex-president of Pakistan. The General is gone and it makes no difference to him but his family will lose the privilege of being the descendent of the president of Pakistan. Whether Bhutto was a martyr or a traitor, as a few call him for being a party for breaking up Pakistan, but his family is having the privilege to rule this nation as long as someone has a mask of his heritage. Benazir has gone but her most ill reputed husband is riding this nation today. Even an under-aged Bilawal is one of those in line aspiring for the presidency or premiership as a matter of right. Unfortunately there is no resistance from Peoples Party's leadership, who apparently have a long line of beneficiaries from this system.

Zia ul Haq's family is unlucky in this respect because the General has been branded as the killer of Mr. Bhutto. Whether he was martyr or 'QATIL' is up to the Court or Khalq-e-Khuda to decide, and Khalqa-e-Khuda is not only the People's Party but also the other overwhelming silent majority that matters. His death punishment was considered to be an extra judicial act because of Zia ul Haq's influence. I cannot help narrating a story when Justice M.R Kiani was Session Judge at District Attock. He acquitted a murderer because of lack of evidence. A few months later the same person was again in his Court for another murder, he was given death punishment. He stood up to address the Judge for a strange justice. He said that he really committed murder last time and was acquitted. This time he had not done it and given death penalty. Justice Kiani smiled and said, "This punishment was actually for the last murder". I wonder which one was Mr. Bhutto's liability: Khawaja Rafique, Dr. Nazir Ahmad, or Nawab Mohammad Ahmad Khan.

Fortunately all dictators (the Generals), have been good enough not to commit the sin which the democrats have been taking pride to groom their own families to keep ruling this poor nation. Mr. Bhutto had the stomach to suggest Air Marshal Asghar Khan to join him rule these illiterate people for good. Air Marshal was gracious enough not to join such a conspiracy against the people of Pakistan. By all means the dictators must be taken to task for their follies but we must also take account of corruption practised openly by so-called innocent civilian democrat angels.

I am an Air Force officer and don't know Gen. Zia ul Haq personally, except that he was a man of courage who could look into the eyes of his enemy and plan well to face him with commitments. In this respect I consider it my right to defend some of the Generals who took over the country under very very odd circumstances prevailing in the country; except Yahiya Khan and Musharaf, who are not defendable and played in the hands of foreign powers or the local civilian politicians and bureaucrats. I am taking this precedence from one of the top lawyer leaders and politician Aitezaz Hassan, who knowing fully well about Zardari's corruption was keen to defend this undefendable character, late Benazir Bhutto, and her Co-partners of NRO fame who had eaten up billions of national money. Even the MQM had advised Zardari to clear his position in the interest of the country. Zia ul Haq had not committed such serious crimes against the nation. I therefore take this opportunity to follow my friend Aitezaz in this sense.

Field Marshal Ayub Khan was invited or ordered by the civilian govt. to impose martial law. His achievements or failures are not my subject, however, it would be fair to leave it to some impartial South Korean, Chinese, or Indonesian historians for his judgment. If we suffice on Mr. Bhutto's dictate, he was ready to constitutionalize him as lifetime president of Pakistan besides accepting him as his own daddy. After Qauid e Azam, Mr. Bhutto is known to be a political prophet by People's Party. They may themselves be the judge to ascertain his above political instinct.

General Zia ul Haq imposed martial law when the country was at the brink of a very serious anarchy due to official rigging in election by Mr. Bhutto's govt. in 1977. There were large scale looting, fires, and rebellion in the country. The junior officers in the Army had refused the command of the seniors and the govt. The opposition's demand for re-election was met with blank refusal by Mr. Bhutto. However, the opposition in a spirit of reconciliation for saving the country brought about a half-hearted agreement but Mr. Bhutto flew away on an unscheduled foreign visit without implementation of the decision. That gave a mixed feeling to the armed forces where General Zia took over as a martial law administrator suspending all political activates in the interim period, which unfortunately took an unusual long time.

His first exploit was to undo undemocratic actions of the democratic govt. of Bhutto, who had banned the National Awami Party (NAP), in Pakistan. And put all his leaders in jail for treason. The General rescued all these leaders from Hyderabad jail and set them free to play politics again in Pakistan. The second obligation was the liberation of Baloch leaders from the clutches of democracy and relieve them to participate in development of their province and their people. The emergency was lifted to allow them to come down from hills to play their role in politics.

In 1979 Soviet Union invasion of Afghanistan created a national crisis in Pakistan with a farsighted Soviet intensions to secure warm water access in Baluchistan. It was imperative to stop the super power lest our coming generations became victim like East Asian countries for a very long time. General Zia ul Haq personally mobilized world Muslim community to physically and financially help Pakistan and Afghanistan to defeat Soviets. Muslims came from all over the world with everything they could muster to fight along with Afghans and Pakistani Mujahiddin. America and Europe chipped-in with money and material. General Zia dealt with America as an equal and bargained with them to his terms and commitments. Ultimately Soviets were defeated, with credit entirely to Zia and Pakistan.

Junejo crisis was another set back for Zia in 1988. During Geneva Accord, when Zia wanted the civilian govt. not to sign any agreement without settlement of Afghan people's govt. fully in command before all the stake holders leave Afghanistan. Junejo govt. displayed an immature behaviour with intentions to get rid of Afghan problem, without assuring international securities. This proved fatal when interim Afghan govt. kept falling one after the other. This indeed concluded that the General was right. This was the main reason for the dismissal of the Junejo's govt. some selfish politicians regard Junejo dismissal as a reprisal of his attitude and deprivation of facilities to the Armed Forces. This aspect was totally fake and amounted to confusing and deceiving the nation as is usually done by the corrupt politicians.

Dealing with India, I think was another feather in his cap. He dealt with India like an enemy deals with the enemy. His Kashmir policy was indeed scary for Indian leadership. His firm policy during Indian Brasstacks operation against Pakistan, in November 1986 invoked well-known cricket diplomacy by Zia ul Haq, which averted adventure by India to invade Pakistan. This was a high-class style of statesmanship to put the enemy in defensive for thinking of any outright war. Rajiv Gandhi, the Indian PM never thought of any such adventure in his lifetime again.

The General was so strong a patriot and shrewd statesman that America had to get rid of him in order to regain control of Pakistan and the associated region again.

After his death my friend Atezaz in collusion with Benazir had to bail out India from Sikh problem where due to their courtesy at least four hundred Sikh leaders were hunted out of their houses by India to quell this insurgency. They also withdrew from supporting Mujahiddin force created by Zia on the Western borders. Indians should be obliged to Benazir and Atezaz from taking off this two pronged pressure from India that damaged the Kashmir issue for all times to come.

Zia ul Haq was a real General and a very shrewd politician who worked for Pakistan and died for this country. His take over as a martial law administrator may be viewed under the local conditions prevailing in the country at that time. His shortcomings and excesses on public liberties cannot be condoned and must be taken account for whatever legal process is available. However, we see that our intellectuals are playing democracy but unfortunately our democracy is promoting corruption in every field of life. This must be taken care of by someone to save the poor masses of Pakistan. We have recently seen judiciary's helplessness in cases of NRO where almost entire democracy is in grip of corruption. Let mid-term election be some kind of scare to these democrats and allow people like Imran Khan and Jamat e Islami take audit of these big parties and decide who is right.

There is also a need to ascertain how many foreign accounts, amount, and property General Zia ul Haq had in foreign countries as compared to civilian leaders like Bhutto, Benazir, Zardari, and Nawaz Sharif to compare the eligibility and right to hold public office and governance of this country.

Learning from History and Holocaust

7ᵗʰ March 2010

History is like a mother who protects her children from impending dangers acquired through her past experience and warns them about recurrence of such insecurities. It also records all events, good or bad, and saves them so that the human beings could learn lesson from their past mistakes and make their lives more pleasant than their forefathers. It is another thing that people learn very little from history and make it a point to repeat those follies again and again to inflict pain and sufferings on themselves. I would like to discuss one of such agonies experienced by us and history keeps reminding about the reaction of common man of today and of those whose forefathers were affected by such misfortunes.

Holocaust was one of the black spots on the Nazi regime during the World War II where almost six million Jews were killed in gas chambers and concentration camps. This was the worst kind of genocide and an act of barbarism by a ruler and his agencies against their own citizens on the basis of religious and sectarian discriminations. The charges against some Jews were collaborating with enemies of Germany during war but collective punishment of all Jews were totally unjustified and did not warrant killing of innocent men women and children. After the war people in the concentration camps and other hiding places that fortunately were not discovered by the Nazis, were rescued by the invading forces. They were then disposed off to different places by the allies to settle them as post-war consequences.

Recently there was 65ᵗʰ anniversary of the Holocaust on the 25ᵗʰ of January 2010, in Israel, Europe, and other countries of Jewish influence. Many speakers delivered the Memorial Day speeches and philosophical thoughts about the happenings with strong applauses by the motivated audience without taking notice of behaviour of Jewish community and Israel on the poor defenceless Palestinians living next door to them, which was no less than the Nazi genocide on Jews and indeed another kind of new Holocaust on Palestinians by Israel.

History warn in her own ways to learn some lesson from the Holocaust that brought misery to the large segment of the Jewish society who suffered through Hitler and his regime and later pushed out of their properties by the honourable West, enblock to Palestine. Unfortunately people who suffered the most through Holocaust are inflicting the same kind of miseries on the Palestinians who provided them with shelter and absorbed them in their society at the cost of their own convenience and comfort. History is watchful of the cruel behaviour of all those settlers with a hidden warning to refrain from the excesses on their benefactors lest one day they might have to face the same kind of torture on them again. The clear message; Take it or leave it, is your prerogative.

Palestinians today are in bigger concentration camps than were Jews in Germany. They have no power to retaliate or even protest against the cruelty of Israel. They have no regular army, no air force, and navy to fight the might of Israel or her allies. They have no power or permission to buy weapons for their defence. Their neighbours have no rights to trade such facilities with them. With the prevailing conditions they envisage no chance to live as equals in this region. It is indeed a mockery of peace talks and two-state theory of America and the West. Unless there is a just solution of Palestine, there could be no peace in the region and many Al Qaedas would keep growing from this fertile land. All money spent on such irrational project will be wasteful. Instead of wasting time on projecting two-state theory, some solid plan may be initiated to unite Palestinians and Jews to live together and present the world an ideal and indeed a real democracy like Whites and Blacks of South Africa.

I can sight an example of the Jewish race in America, which I personally saw during my visit in 1956. Jews were one of the forbidden segments of the US society. Honourable American families considered it below their dignity to have any relations with the then Jewish families. Today they are equal partners or even superior to common Whites in social and business status. When you mix up people with each other, the merit grows and development of society takes place in all aspects. No one is in loss; everybody gained from education, ideas, intellect, resources and joint ventures. So was the case with Blacks and today they have a Black president in America. It was the greatness of American people and a brave fight of Blacks for their rights to bring this change. Jews in Israel must follow their masters, the Americans, and accept a new life of collaboration to develop Palestine for all people living there now. They have to initiate, as they are more powerful and resourceful in every field today. They must throw the old Nazi hatred of Jews, which gave no advantage to ordinary Germans of that time but instead pushed them away from other races and countries of Europe and Russia.

Post World War II scenario in Europe was very interesting and inquisitive. Every country wanted to bring their original system and governance back on track. However, according to me the combined consensus was to get rid of Jews from Europe. Switzerland was the only exception. They all got together to transport them to Palestine. Whether common Jews agree or not, this was another way of confirming Hitler's action that Jews were undesirable elements to live in Europe, otherwise they should have been embraced and compensated for their sufferings and allowed to establish themselves at places where they belonged before war. By pushing them out to Palestine meant getting rid of them once and for all. Hitler was only guilty for doing the same thing through coercive and brute manners. This would have been an eye opener for them to realize where they really stood and had given them the insight to strive to live with Palestinians as equal partners.

The Jews were welcomed and accepted with open heart by Palestinians who felt that they had suffered at the hands of Europeans, the highly civilized society. Critically and technically this was no less than a Holocaust to force or persuade a large segment of people out of their own countries so far from their homes from where they had no chance to come back. The history was watching this reality by seeing Jews rushing to Israel from all over the world.

This wilful accommodation of Jews by the Palestinians was blatantly misused by the Jews who bought the lands from the local poor people by intent or deceit and turned them out of the area by force. A time came when most of the lucrative land was owned by Jews who organized a real fighting force due courtesy and support of masters in Europe who had felt guilty of throwing them out of their own countries. The Jews really behaved like an Arab camel that forced the real occupants out of their tents by establishing a country called Israel.

Humiliations of day-to-day dealings by Israel brings a feeling of disgrace and indignity which increases hatred against Jews. Every now and then bombing by F-16 fighters on the unarmed empty-handed people gives a sense of helplessness and outrage against Israel. Killing one of the most prominent Hamas blind leader, Sheikh Ahmad Yaseen, by air attack while he was going for prayer to the mosque was no less than Holocaust. Putting Chairman Yasir Arafat under house arrest for almost two years (2002-2004), who died on 24th Nov-04, while he was still in confinement. Such incidents are killing the soul of Palestinians and no Holocaust is severest than this.

Barrack Hussein Obama seems a messiah today to initiate settlement of Palestinian issue judiciously through pressure by American Jews and his government. This itself will eliminate major element of terrorism in the world that has spread to Iraq, Afghanistan, Pakistan, and elsewhere due to basically the same source. The solution will provide a beacon of light to everyone to solve their mutual differences in a civilized manner.

Nelson Mandela is the proud witness of history. He forgave those who declared him a terrorist and tortured his entire nation for centuries. He gave away his presidency voluntarily and became immortal. I urge Palestinians to forgive Israel provided they learn from this accord of history. Their forefathers were tortured by Nazis but they have no right to force the same kind of Holocaust on poor Palestinians. If we believe that history repeats itself, we must accept that coercive treatment to Palestinians are actually inviting another Salahudddin Ayubi to repeat the history and send them back from where they came. Let it be known to them all that time is no constraint on such established principles.

A Foreign Land in Lahore

7ᵗʰ March 2010

It would not be appropriate to regard it a pleasant surprise but it was certainly an unusual experience to visit a place that totally gave a foreign independent look where Pakistani Law was apparently not visible. Entry to this land was restricted to only the foreigners and elites of Pakistan (who were practically no less than foreigners). I was indeed astonished to visit a kind of foreign land within the boundaries of Lahore city limits.

A friend of mine was invited to dinner and through his courtesy I happened to join the party. This foreign territory was called Royal Palm Club, situated on the Canal Bank short of old Griffan Club of Railways. I was told it was sold on lease by Gen. Musharaf's Railway Minister, Gen (R) Javed Qazi, at throw away price to presumably a foreign party (I don't know the name and not sure of his nationality). We took about an hour to travel a distance of about two miles. It appeared as if ¼ of Lahore was rushing to this territory with a sudden thrill. On reaching the territorial limits of the place we faced extremely difficult and demanding security checks before entering the outer gates. A further security check and direction took us to inner limits of nobility. Passing through some very elegant tables and beautiful gentry we were taken out to delightfully decorated veranda where our hosts were sitting with closely lit braziers.

We were very warmly received by the host and his two friends having Arabian style puffs of Hukkah with a long snake like pipe. It really presented look of a crowd of Arab Sheiks sitting at the footpath at Edgware Road London in the evening hours of enjoyment. A few more tables with the same style presented a look of an aristocratic elegance and occupants with pipes in their mouths and making intentionally crooked distorted lips and faces were indeed amusing. The smoke of braziers, hukka, and pipes gave a very pleasant smell of scented tobacco.

A stylish waiter came to take our order for drinks. The host were having wine and whisky, we ordered the same. I made the mistake of asking what kind of Scotch they had. I wanted to impress the host with my choice of Shiva's Regal. He took all my air out by saying they didn't serve cheap stuff and asked about the choice from Royal Salute and Blue Label. From then on I remained defensive for the rest of the evening for lack of knowledge of such high-class names of drinks and food, which my countrymen were proud to possess. I sheepishly enquired whom this land belonged to. The friend of our host almost took an exception to my question and asked if this was my first visit. He said this place belonged to some x, y, z but people like Tariq Ali, a Pakistani born Londoner intellectual, Wajid Shamsul Hassan, Qamer Kahira, Zardari, and Yousuf Salauddin type grace the place almost everyday. I again asked an awkward question if Nawaz or Shahbaz Sharif were allowed to enter here. He shook his head in affirmative but smiled that since no "lassi and paey" are served, they avoid coming here.

During our pleasant moments of sitting I saw quite a bit of hustle bustle and presence of good looking females with strange dress like aliens and escorted by even strange looking males with jeans and upper garments reflecting a completely unknown exotic genes. My innocence or ignorance was soon noticed by our host who explained that these strange looking habitants belonged to an international fashion show in the adjacent hall. I was really demoralized to learn that each table reservation cost at least 2 to 5 lakh Rupees for the show. I not only felt depressed but also inferiority complex amongst such a high-class elite or filthy rich crowd who had no value for money in a poor country like Pakistan. Since it was like a foreign territory I ignored it as one of that society which is of no concern to us commoners.

I was now beginning to realize that it was really a club in Pakistan and under a legitimate rule of law of Pakistan. My host were fed up of my questions when I objected to openly serving of alcohol against the law of the land. They had no answer to this, however, my next question that in a sensitive place like this surely there would be at least twenty intelligence agents to watch this highly distinguished crowd and their activities against Pakistan. Our host laughed sarcastically and revealed that most of them must be drinking on club account and exchanging views with management before sending it to their Head Quarters. I couldn't confirm such revelation but felt embarrassed from inside to learn about my country's security reporting procedure.

It was time to eat and we all shifted inside the hall to have a comfortable and warm environment for delightful treat. The food was exquisite and so was the crowd in the hall. It really increased our appetite and I made full use of the uninvited invitation. My friend and myself left our hosts gratefully and I of course had a strange feeling of being in Pakistan and abroad at the same time.

KHUDA WANDA YE TEREY SADA DIL BANDEY KITHER JAEIN

KE DARVESHY BHI AYARI HAY SULTANI BHI AYARI

"Oh God where should we simple people go; because the whole world is full of duplicity"

Strategic Dialogue with America

30ᵗʰ March 2010

To me strategic dialogues are basically a cunning exchange of views between political friends with new promises. It amounts to point scoring over one another and repairing cracks on quality of trust or to bridge the gap occurred since the last meeting.

America and Pakistan have been striving to develop some such understanding in fighting terrorism in Afghanistan, tribal areas bordering Pakistan/Afghanistan and its spread deep inside Pakistan. People in Pakistan are keenly watching its outcome to a new plan of action to deal with the situation. I am sure the people of United States are also watching the development in the same spirit. Many more such dialogues would be planned in future till some final settlement is reached.

We have been fighting this war along with American and NATO allies for the last eight years. Ever since Gen. Musharaf surrendered to Mr. Bush's telephone call and accepted his dictation, we have been going from bad to worse in this war. Americans have been spending almost one billion Dollars every month, and Pakistan battling multiple fronts in Swat, South Waziristan and suicidal attacks deep inside its cities. The new American government must realize that, the philosophy of friends not masters is the only lasting relationship. If authoritative doctrine had not been applied and war not forced down the throat of Pakistan, an amicable plan could have formulated with mutual consent, we could have saved eight years of war, loss of precious lives, and tremendous amount of money that could have been used for reviving the economy of Afghanistan and Pakistan. Both, people of Pakistan and America would be sitting at open restaurants and enjoying their meals discussing mutual interests. Big or small, friends have an equal status and deal with each other in the same spirit.

This was the fourth strategic dialogue between the two countries but this one had a special significance because of the level at which it was being discussed. Both sides had come prepared with various proposals, to leave some and accept some to demonstrate visible achievements to their respective countries. Unfortunately the American govt. always attaches Indian involvement necessary for every solution in this region.

Where does India stand in strategic dialogue between Pakistan and America? Everyone is aware in Pakistan that Indian Foreign and Interior Minister were specially called to America for briefing and advise on dialogue with Pakistan a week before. Are American officials totally naive that a 'friend's enemy' is no forum, which can honestly deliberate about their problems. India is being intentionally involved in Afghanistan to neutralize Pakistan in the region. Firstly She is in no position to perform this task because of her location and secondly we shall never allow her to do that. Afghanistan is purely Pakistan's problem, and both Afghanistan and Pakistan can mutually sort out their problems with American help in the long run.

Americans have to slightly go back to December 1979 to appreciate the situation when Soviets invaded Afghanistan. On initiation from Pakistan, Muslims from all over the world rushed to Pakistan to face Soviet onslaught. Let it be known to the world that it were only the Muslim Jihadis who defeated the Soviet Union. All other elements including America and Europe only chipped-in in terms of equipment and money. India was friend of Soviet and she played that role with all its resources and influence without any hesitation, however, it did not create any dent in the victory of Muslims. India is therefore in no position to change anything in Afghanistan today. This is a point to ponder for the American think tanks that the war is fought and won standing with friends only.

We, in Pakistan are interested in American exit strategy from Afghanistan and as friends will ensure their safe and pleasant departure. Modalities may be one of the points to be discussed in the strategic dialogues. India has no role to play in this scenario and I hope the American think tanks for once have a rational perception. India and Pakistan are not friends and shall remain so as long as Kashmir problem is not solved. American behaviour in the past had been encouraging Indian supremacy over

Pakistan which dragged Pakistan to match Indian nuclear capability. This issue should be a logical entry in any future dialogue.

Pakistan's political and economical stability is the guarantee to settle Afghan situation. A prosperous Pakistan is key for stable Afghanistan in future. Pakistan is the frontline ally and has been the strongest partner against war on terror. She has suffered the most in this war and that also because of America, as a friend or through intimidation. However, things have changed and now our relationship rests in friendship only. We need to be compensated for the loss we have suffered. 1.5 billion dollars per year is no compensation. It is only a day-to-day rations. We really need to get away with our debts to start afresh, reconstitute our energy shortage and reconstruct our industry, which is totally ruined because of American war and now our own.

Whosoever has initiated these strategic dialogues, it might be able to clarify some issues and straighten a few futuristic plans between friends. Let us hope the new dialogues help us change the cunning exchange of views into honest intentions to work together to end this operation and any future conflict in the best interest of American, Pakistan, and Afghanistan.

Nuclear Security Summit 2010

23rd April 2010

We welcome the big leaders of the world, claiming to represent six billion people exploring peaceful living for them in the above summit, but they must also take into account a few millions whose grievances go beyond their personal control to indulge in criminal activities including terrorism. This overwhelming majority must realise the plight of the few aggrieved suffering through the courtesy and exploits of this honourable majority. Peace comes with prosperity and justice all around. Selective approach of adjustments for a purposeful reason leads to disappointments and bitterness. Fairness is the name of the game. Favours to some at the cost of the others breeds imbalance and must be stopped. 'Running with Hare and hunting with hounds' is not acceptable to the world of today.

Barak Hussein Obama was my dream president. His election campaign; his speeches and the feeling that we got out of him were indeed honourable and virtuous. We in the third world expected a big change from America and when Obama pledged the change we all believed him and I am sure the American people did the same. However, subsequent events disappointed the international community to a large extent. Iraq is still burning, Afghanistan in the grip of uncertainty, Pakistan on the brink of terrorism and victim of drone attacks, Iran heading towards severe sanctions. Kashmir is left at the mercy of time. What can summit do to the relation between nuclear India and Pakistan? These questions are connected to these vital small problems, which is most vulnerable for nuclear proliferation. Above all the Israeli monster is everyday at the door of Palestinian playing havoc and the spectators at the summit are watching and hiding themselves for face saving. No summit can guarantee nuclear safety unless these small but crucial problems are taken care off.

Today's giants are an advanced, educated and the most civilized society yet when it comes to their personal concern and passion they tend to forego all magnanimity and teachings and opt for a merciless revenge. We have seen it practised by a super power to a very poor country like Afghanistan after 9/11. In lieu of three thousand dead and loss of property they killed at least one million and razed the country to Stone Age with fifty seven thousand air-craft destructive sorties; and have yet not forgiven them after ten years but intend to continue for further unlimited period. Destroyed Iraq with war and sanctions by killing one and a half million men, women, and innocent children with merely a future alarm of threat to America and Israel. I sometimes wonder how different is this society from Genghis Khan, Halaku Khan, and Taimur Ling of Dark ages.

This was a unique summit with almost forty heads of states, and a few very high officials representing their governments. Israeli head of state was intentionally let off not to attend to save her and the United States of the embarrassment of facing the truth and providing an excuse to Iran for following with the same finesse. The presence of countries like Armenia, Singapore, and UAE, was very intriguing. Perhaps Vatican could have been a better choice. Absence of Iran and North Korea was conspicuously felt because of their rebellion to the United States. An unnecessary suspicion haunts us all for the future of these two countries and I personally hope that the big brothers are not thinking of a Stone Age treatment for them like that of Afghanistan and Iraq. This solution might take another twenty years of turmoil and tremendous loss of life and destruction in the world. We pray that a better solution be found to save the world.

China is a country of straight and honest politics whose leadership has practically demonstrated sincerity and sharing of resources for the benefit of others. Their behaviour has been fair and positively understood by the world so far, except with an odd example of India who needs to look inside herself. The same image can be displayed by other big countries to make a summit like this more effective and meaningful. However, if Chinese have to earn respect and keep it lasting they have to protect the interest of small and poor countries in their orbit. If America can put all her weight behind Israel, China must keep the balance with Iran. This is but natural and I am sure must be on Chinese future agenda. The summit and the so-called strategic dialogues are nothing but the dreams and we all know dreams are seldom a reality.

Summit like this can only be effective if the super power keeps equation between countries unbiased irrespective of their size and economic effects. Countries like India and China probably can deal with each other without the outside interference, but India and Pakistan must be dealt with differently. Similarly Israel and Iran have different proportions. Personal interest should not be hidden under the carpet to pave the way for spurious reconciliations between them and the super power. Conduit relationship might be desirable for a better future between the big and small countries. Deliberately ignoring important partners like Iran and Korea is like intentionally keeping the smoke under the rug.

Summits are like pathfinders, the more one deliberates the more one is led to the right direction. Patience is the best treatment for heading to a correct destination. This summit ended with a note of acceptance by all concerned and unconcerned to safeguard the nuclear material from getting into wrong hands. The apparent consensus rested on Al Qaeda but arresting Al Qaeda was not even discussed. It is difficult to cure a disease without the correct diagnosis. Muslims and the extremists are not the cause for existence of Al Qaeda. It is the **Israel**! Open deliberation might lead you to the peaceful solution of the problem. The next summit might be the right venue to go deep into this troubled water and find the truth. However, no one prohibits ongoing efforts to deal with Al Qaeda and other extremists.

All powerful and prominent leaders of today may like to follow Nasir Kazmi, a compassionate Urdu language poet:

"Koi Andhi Na Bujaey Kissi Muflis Ka Chiragh
Dosto Aisi Koi Rasam Bhi Daali Jaeey"

[O Friends! Let us establish a tradition (kindle a light) where no storm can extinguish this flame of the poor in future].

American withdrawal from Afghanistan

17ᵗʰ May 2010

It is a general belief that sliding down a ditch is easy, but getting out of it is indeed a back breaking process. When 9/11 provoked Americans to fulfil their national obligation to revenge from Al Qaida, they decided to attack Afghanistan where a few Al-Qaida people along with their leader Osama bin laden was operating. Without going into the past history of Afghanistan, Mr. Bush made an immediate decision to attack. The sitting government of Taliban were highly disorganised with no regular army and air force to face a foreign aggression. One of their rivals, the Northern alliance holding about 20% of the country was in a rebellious state from the central government. They were instigated and directed to attack the main land to take over the country. In spite of Pakistan's efforts to withhold this operation, Mr. Bush urged them to force their way to Kabul with enormous Air force support. In fact this was one of the biggest air force operations with fifty seven thousand sorties of strategic-bombers and fighter-bombers with the most modern weapons. Carpet-bombing and senseless use of force on a country having no power of retaliation and resistance was launched to see the effectiveness of the new weapons on human shields and mountains.

The difficult and rugged terrain, the very rough and tough tribals of Afghanistan known to be one of the bravest and wild fighters in the world had the capacity to fight with empty stomach for unimaginable period. The war on paper looked very easy and simple because of the existing weak statistics of the Taliban. Mr. Bush was not in a position to ask the Russians but he could have certainly consulted the British before embarking on this adventure. They had plenty of experience of the Afghans and the terrain because of their campaigns in eighteen and nineteen centuries. American think tanks with all their knowledge and research could have been handy if they were seriously premeditated. I think Mr. Bush was in a hurry to record his name in the American history as the one who could perform the impossible.

The war is on for the last ten years and there seems no end of the tunnel. Pakistan has also been involved by force and now there are at least fifteen countries America, British, all NATO counties, Afghanistan and Pakistan fighting hand full of Talibans hiding inside Afghanistan and the Tribal Areas of Pakistan. The survival of Taliban with no source of income, no production of weapon, no money to buy them, no ration even to eat is a matter of surprise and point to ponder for all of us and the American think tanks. A few off hand analysis and reasoning to justify their resistance is mostly rubbish and should be thrown in to gutters. Each and every citizen of Afghanistan is a Taliban from inside when it comes to face invaders and while drawing the correct deductions one has to take into account at least twenty million of these warriors and their tactics.

Surrender and defeat are very harsh and disgraceful terms even to think of, especially by the super power and other most modern allies. However honourable retreat is a sensible proceeding by any worldly standards. The British won the World War II from Germany but had to leave the bases and colonies on whose strength they had achieved this victory. After the war they realized that they had to leave. They retreated from India (the golden sparrow), the Middle East and Africa one by one and squeezed themselves in the small island across the English Channel. However, they established a common wealth of all these countries who willingly and happily bade farewell to them and are still a kind of integral part of the British Empire. A few millions opted to shift to England and were welcomed by the local population and are now absorbed by this small country as British subjects. That credit also goes to America who accepted some of the Japanese, Koreans and Vietnamese. I am sure they have not created any problem for Americans, rather contributing in economic growth. Such lesson from history should not be set aside but followed in future also.

A pleasant retreat is required by America to save her honour and people and accept an agreeable and memorable farewell while leaving Afghanistan. However it cannot be free of charge. To shed off something one has to make some sacrifices in lieu.

The other day in one of my hallucinations I saw Mr. Obama sitting with his key politicians and generals outside the lawns of the White house to finalise the plans of the solution of war in Afghanistan. Most of the generals were in favour of let out & leave but after paying adequate damages to appease the majority of Afghans to keep relationship alive for future. Some suggested that the people were the Taliban's, who should be the one as part of the decision making from Afghan side and not Karzai's party. Almost all of them wanted Pakistan as part of the proceedings to represent from both sides. Politicians on the contrary had a very diverse discussion. Some were against Pakistan because of the terrorist activities and extremism. A few favouring Pakistan for putting her in this situation. Some very strong looking argued about Iran's negative role in pursuing their nuclear assets. Some were very emphatic that India would be unhappy and may adopt indifferent posture not suiting American interest visa wiz Chinese status in this part of the world. Not one person talked about the American loss of lives, economic ruination and Pakistan's total destruction in every field of life. As a soldier myself it was indeed very painful to listen to these gentlemen who were totally unmindful of the poor people who had actually brought them to this position of authority.

Barak Hussain Obama broke his silence with the remarks that if he followed his politician friends it might take a few more years to see the end which might be too late for all of us. With his responsibility towards people and their welfare he would like Generals to come out with some solid suggestions to get out of this dangerous situation.

A General rose with a carrot & stick. A Politician remarked that this man sounded like Condoleezza Rice. The General said such matters always ended with only these two weapons, a carrot & a stick. As a goodwill gesture we should offer good Afghans an incentive of immigrating to United State. He remarked that there was nothing to worry as there would be many not willing to migrate because of their tribal traditions. Secondly he was not aware if any afghan was ever involved in any terrorist activities in United State.

It was contemplated by all to arrange a composite dialogue between Pakistan, Taliban, other Afghan leadership & America. Pakistan is assigned to coordinate and create an environment of peace and new relationship between the parties. Other options may be considered to include in the forum to make it more effective. With a positive approach and new connections with the Taliban a ceremonial parade by all combined forces be announced with cessation of hostilities and beginning of new era. No more drone attacks on tribal areas of Pakistan and general amnesty for all Pakistani and Afghan based Talibans. The other modalities to be settled as combined strategies by the UNO and other agencies, as decided by the concerned parties.

I suddenly found myself amongst these elite with all eyes pouncing on me implying their achievement for establishing democracy in Afghanistan. To me this was the biggest lie and I had to retaliate frankly with my personal experience about my wish to become a fighter pilot. All my instructors failed to accomplish this because I had no aptitude to make a fighter pilot. Tribal society has its own traditions which they follow religiously. They strictly speaking have no aptitude for this at the moment and one cannot force this down their throats. This will suite only Karzai and Party who want corruption for people of their own breed. The people of Afghanistan might change like earlier British, German, and French had done; and the Russians are doing now. Time is at their disposal and light of the education is slowly creeping around the globe. They have to receive it in their own time. The brutal democracy enforced in Iraq is as fragile. The moment occupying forces leave they will return to their former state within one to two years time. I served in Iraq on deputation for three years during 1968-71 and speak of my personal evaluation and observation of the Iraqi society. The present democracy has been taking toll of about 200 people, on the average every day since its illegitimate start and people are fed up with this democracy of devilish disposition.

I was wondering if Obama was really in control of things in convening this meeting to resolve the ongoing problems that he inherited from his superior race. I got up with a big thud and found myself talking to the American think tanks to work for their fellow human beings and not for Politicians and self seekers who tend to take advantage of their intellectual abilities.

YE DUNIA RAHAY NA RAHAY MERAY HAMDAM

KAHANI MOHABBAT KI ZINDA RAHAY GI

(My friend this world may survive or not; the love will live forever)

Desire to befriend India
(Aman ki Asha)

11ᵗʰ June 2010

Peace is a symbol of prosperity; it promotes goodwill, brings about developments with an invisible pleasure in the lives of individuals in the environments they are living. They start enjoying as partners to each other in delight and distress. This is what we both in Pakistan and India really need to examine and get rid of unpleasant events of our past history. However, protective rights and achievements make things difficult at individual and collective levels. An honest analysis becomes difficult when it involves self-seekers with total disregard to the overall advantage of the communities. Selfish trait supersedes all logical reasoning and animal instinct over-powers all humanitarian characteristics. Doctrine of elimination of the weak by the powerful takes precedence over everything.

This principle of elimination is unfortunately a reality. I am neither a student of history, nor a person of philosophical thoughts; I am simply a devout observer and a nationalist. What ever comes in my way, in my own capacity, like to pass it on to my countrymen? I feel I am obligated to disseminate such facts irrespective of likes or dislikes for the sake of genuine peace between India and Pakistan. My national instinct forces me to reach out to our think tanks and intellectual's desire to cement good relations with India or even graft back the portion fallen apart through the will of Muslim minority of India.

In our day to day village life when a big landlord finds a poor farmer settling down in his neighbourhood, he tries all immoral methods to eliminate him or make him run away from there. Similar is the case between big and small businessmen. The big one tries to buy-out the small one unless the principle of perseverance is practiced by the underdogs to stay put at all cost. The big states behave exactly in the same fashion with the smaller neighbours. The case of Sikkim, Nepal, and Bhutan, is a good example. We certainly wouldn't like to follow the suit and give up all our rights and accept to live with them for the sake of a few traders and landlords, created by British to rule India. We would love to live with them as equals, with self-respect and pride as a sovereign nation.

India is a big neighbour. We like to learn from her and utilize our resources together for the benefit of our's and their masses. We, on our part have tried all methods to befriend in the past and live happily together for the sake of poor people living under poverty levels in both countries. We have so far failed to put any dent into the hard-core leadership of India. We have certainly made mistakes in the process but I think always tried to makeup to normalize the relations. However, the big brother is still not convinced and is using all kind of immoral methods to cripple us through economic pressures, water deprivation from Kashmir rivers and political isolation in the world. We either adopt the process of perseverance or succumb to the pressure. The price has to be negotiated no matter how long it takes to conclude. We are both sailing in the same boat, safety of which is our mutual responsibility.

India needs peace as much as we in Pakistan are craving for. The size is totally immaterial as a deciding factor. Realization of this by India is the only hope for reconciliation. Aman ki Asha is quite different than the Aman (peace) itself. Our elites who are dying for peace must understand that peace does not come by begging or accruing some benefits and personal gains for them. It comes with sharing of views and feelings for each other. I have no doubt that the masses of both sides are dying for it but those holding the charge are not following the same directions. General Musharaf tried his best by showering so many options but India never ever commented officially on any one of the concessions. They were waiting for more discount and acceptance of their point of views. Thank God Musharaf could not hold his office to see the ultimate. We all would be regretting for the rest of our lives.

We have made plenty of sacrifices already to live in peace but could not realize our big brother's appetite to his satisfaction. We let go Junaghar to his way, kept quiet on Hyderabad, accepted seas-fire on Kashmir when we had an upper hand. We had to bear disgrace in East Pakistan by giving away half of our country and degrading ourselves from one of the top strategic force to a small position of irrelevance in the world. However, it appears that no amount of sacrifice will suffice except total submission to our big brother. We have to decide if we were ready to go this far for the sake of peace and prosperity. We also had a very painful experience in Afghanistan and Baluchistan because of the role of Indian interference and its effects. In 1962 during India China conflict in Northern areas, Pakistan displayed extreme constraint and tolerance in-spite of having a favourable chance to settle score over Kashmir; like India attacked Hyderabad while we were mourning the death of our Father of the Nation in 1948.

Srilanka once decided to follow that path and requested India for assistance to establish peace in their country in 1960's. They had to fight for thirty long years to washout their request from the big neighbour. Who doesn't know that Tamil Tigers were the brainchild of India and were nourished and fed with all kind of help through Tamil Nados of India to break away from Srilanka. I think our elite force of peace-mongers may like to solicit with the brave sons of Srilanka to know the reality of the 'Aman ki Asha'. Our peacemakers must learn the importance of perseverance from Srilanka.

India has already decided its terms for peace and is giving us time for acceptance. They have declared Kashmir as 'Attoot Ang', and made it a part of their constitution. Azad Kashmir is on their list as disputed territory with Pakistan. And they want it to be on their agenda item for the peace talks. They have made a fairly large number of small barrages and big dams in occupied Kashmir for development of agriculture and power generation. It would be a folly to imagine that they were doing all this to hand it over to Kashmiris or Pakistan as a good will gesture to make friends. However, piety has no bounds and a few kind gestures for a younger brother would certainly help to live together with the same old relations as the same people.

On our part, we certainly want peace and friendship with India. We like people of India especially their poor and our poor masses' prosperity as the basis of our relationship and friendship. We want to celebrate their colourful functions and hug them to demonstrate our love and sympathy, but we want some reciprocation for all the sacrifices we have made for goodwill. Kashmir is a vital and core issue in our differences. Aman ki Asha, must have a loud cry that Kashmir is no one's Atoot Ang, and must be solved on the basis of the free will of Kashmiris. That would be the first whisper of Mst Asha, if we have to live together as friends, otherwise it is simply futile exercise of travel and tourism by the self seekers and traders. Desire for peace is a very noble instinct and an honest reciprocity is equally important otherwise the whole proceeding will become irrelevant and counter productive. Manmohan Singh is a weak and meek PM, and so is Soniya Gandhi for the reasons well known to her and most of the Indian leadership. You really need a person like Vajpayee, Jaswant Singh, or LK Adwani, to follow Aman ki Aasha, from Indian side. The gap between us must be narrowed and ultimately filled with both sides inching equally from both ends to meet in the middle. Only one-way movement might fall into a mistrust ditch with a long recovery period at the end of the show.

"Mohabbat dono janib ho to barhti hai

Wagarna ghut ke mar jati hai sapnon mein"

(The love excels only if both sides are equally edging towards each other, otherwise it is forgotten like a dream)

The Future of Pakistan

1ˢᵗ August 2010

Believe me the future of Pakistan is in safe hands. This is my faith and it stands firm like the sun rises from the East and it does not change in spite of all the recent set-backs. I am surely not talking about Zardari's dirty, or Gilani's trembling hands; nor Nawaz Sharif's fragile or Altaf Hussains remote control hands. It is not even Munarwar Hassan and Imran Khan's clean hands that matter under the prevailing situation. Yet I am sure like death that some invisible divine hands who created this country are keeping it under his own protection and trust.

1947 was a very crucial moment when thousands of refugees from India were pouring in without any subsistence, no funds available to support the infra structure, most of the army and equipment lying in enemy territory, no suitable civil offices facilities, no police available for security, civil bureaucracy hardly visible to run the country, and clerical staff without even paper pins to run day to day routine work. Our enemies declared a few days target for our existence. Yet Pakistan survived with dignity and self-assurance to make place in the world community as a viable important state. Even in those harsh and critical days we managed to win over Azad Kashmir, and forced our strong neighbour to run to the United Nations for seize fire. With this excuse they occupied the other portion of Kashmir by deception. However, since then they never had any doubt about our existence in their neighbourhood.

The founder of the Nation departed in very critical moments when we were beginning to stabilize and pick up a fresh start. This was a grave setback but we recovered and continued a competitive race along with our neighbour. In order to survive in such hostile environments, our new leadership had to take a few unwanted political decisions in 1950's, but it certainly gave us the confidence to face the prevailing situation in the region. Joining SEATO and CENTO along with American Military aid, could be unwise but I think was important against the satanic Indian Soviet collision.

1960's saw a new turn when the Indian metal started melting in the wake of our well-established military and industrial progress. This indirectly gave rise to a destructive jealousy from our neighbour who backed out of her obligations on the disputed territory of Kashmir with new excuses of our military alliances with America and the West. This brought a new wave of hatred amongst the people and subsequently violent actions in the bordering areas of Azad and occupied Kashmir resulted in a full-fledged war in the two neighbouring countries in 1965.

Pakistan though one third of the Indian military strength proved too strong for India to swallow. Indians were beaten on almost all fronts in the ground battle. Pakistan Airforce beat her adversary in the skies and in the support of ground forces. PAF had complete air superiority in seventeen days of war till India was rescued again by the UNO. This gave the world, specially the West, a new dimension towards Pakistan and its importance in the region.

After 1965 war with India, the Americans and the West realized the potential of Pakistan Armed Forces. They specially got alarmed when all the Muslim counties in the Middle East accepted Pakistan as a leader and wanted them to reorganize their Armed Forces. This would have boosted Pakistan's economy and political image over already established forces in the area. With Indonesia's Sukarno, a staunch ally of Pakistan at that time, the West could not bear to lose almost entire Middle East and South East Asia from their influence.

Under instigation from Israel, the Americans and the West could not ignore Pakistan's supremacy and excel in this region. Americans blamed Pakistan for using their weapons against India, and subsequently stopped all spare support and replenishment of war losses. The West totally cooled down on all on-going development projects by curtailing all trade facilities to Pakistan. We knocked at China's door, but it was almost impossible to cover the deficiencies created by our western friends.

In order to please India and to reduce Pakistan's developing strength our American allies and the West decided to break Pakistan through ethnic and provincial differences from within; at the same time encouraging India to strike when the iron was hot. India with the help of Soviet Union and connivance of western friends were able to humiliate Pakistan by defeating her in East Pakistan with the help of our own people revolting in 1971. Pakistan was broken with East Pakistan renamed as Bangladesh and West Pakistan a new Pakistan. The new Pakistan though cut into half the size yet became stronger than the old one. It defaced Soviet Union in 1989 in Afghanistan and became nuclear power in 1998 to become at power with India with all times to come. India, which claimed superiority over full Pakistan, was now in no position to face nuclear Pakistan Militarily. This is one of the reasons for her flirtation with America to regain the same old position of conventional days. It would not be out of place to mention that Bangladesh today is like a second Pakistan in the overall partition of the subcontinent.

Pakistan remains intact in spite of all efforts by external and internal enemies to destroy it. Indian American collusion, Afghan terrorist activists and Soviet efforts to eliminate and take precedence over one another to be in front line when it disintegrates. I bet it would remain an unpleasant dream for all of them like all those who had wished to do it in the past. Indra Ghandi, Mujeeb ur Rehman, Bhutto and their families met terrible fate for being party of breaking up of this God given gift to the Muslims of the Subcontinent. The others who wish to provoke the nature again may face the same fate accompli.

Americans are already facing the music in Iraq and Afghanistan. NATO seems to be next on the list; Turkey would be the first to put the nail in its coffin. She is the oldest member of the NATO but not yet allowed to enter the European Union because she bears the name of Islam. The flood of the ex-protégées of Soviet Union maybe the other torrent in the way of its end.

India should realize the problems emanating out of Afghan crisis. Their leadership should refrain from cashing out of a volatile situation by creating misunderstandings between Pakistan, America, and the West. Her interference in Baluchistan shall not fulfil her desire and dream of the same result as of Bangladesh. She must fulfil her obligation on

Kashmir like on honourable country dreaming to become member of the Security Council.

England is party to Kashmir dispute and should act neutral in relations with both India and Pakistan. In a recent visit to India, Prime Minister, **David Cameron**, behaved like an ordinary village bully taking sides of the benefactor. England does not need to provide her shoulder to India to cry, against Pakistan. Neither she needs to sell her principles so cheap to earn one billion pounds for the sale of hawk trainers to India. India though is a big market but one doesn't have to put their basic values on sale for a few chips. However, **Mr. Cameron** may go all out to humour India but he is not going to secure the facilities from Hindu mentality what the East India Company got from a Muslim Emperor Jahangir of India in 1612. It may sound crude but the basic ingredients of character do not change. No one knows this more than the British who were particular not to recruit a menial Indian soldier in their army. The Prime Minister of Britain should not lose balance on seeing a small sum of money within his reach. He should have realized that where he was standing was a place of massive terrorism against Muslims by the Indian state and their agents sometime back.

Pakistan has come to stay till the end of the world. All efforts to destroy her before would result in self-destruction of those who wish to do it. India may learn from Soviets and from her own history of fighting with Muslims. We want to befriend India for the sake of both countries poor masses and relationship of mutual inheritance. The future of Pakistan is in safe hands and anyone who wants to destroy her shall meet the same fate in consequence from the power that created her.

Self-execution through Foreign Loans

29ᵗʰ August 2010

The world financial organizations are on the lookout to extend loans to countries facing problems due natural disaster or other difficulties and need financial assistance to cope up with the unusual situation. They also remain in contact with corrupt officials of the governments who are keen to make money in such national emergencies. In the event of crises they activate their agents to persuade their governments to acquire loans from these agencies. This is one of the reasons why our present government is pouncing on the foreign loans. The interested powers conspire to expose Pakistan under the burden of foreign loans and drive towards a failed state. We have to learn to live under hard ship and face calamities like earthquakes and floods ourselves. That is the only way we shall prove our firmness and maturity in this competitive world with dignity and resolution. The World Bank, the Asian Development Bank, and IMF shower easy loans to accrue benefit through heavy interest. This is a trap to lead us to an unending begging trend that makes our standing incredible in the world community and sacrifice our independent foreign policy with all the financial strength in the hands of others.

The present floods in the country have broken the back of the people in almost every province but could not take away the will that nourishes self-respect. Hunger and suffering kills a man many times before his actual death. One can bear his own pain but cannot see the pain of his women and children. In such catastrophe leaders are the one who provide shoulder to common man facing these sufferings but unfortunately they run away to foreign countries instead of giving hands to their people in trouble.

2005 earthquake gave us a sudden shock that shook the nation by surprise. The entire northern area of Pakistan was affected, some with total destruction and the rest under death trap because of the total damage of the ground communication. The only way to reach people was through air, which was not possible with available internal resources. Our friends around the world were keen to reach with every

196

possible help. The entire nation from Karachi to Peshawar was on their feet to rush to the affected areas. Those who could manage ground transportation were lined up on the roads with all the support material. Those who could trust their legs were running to reach their distressed countrymen. The foreign friends were so kind that they came with everything, cash, helicopters, doctors, nurses, and eating material that we could hardly manage to absorb. It was indeed more than the required to meet the emergency. We are still having some of the surpluses with us unutilized even today. Some of the stuff is still being sold in the local markets after so many years. Our government yet opted to secure loan from world monitory organizations in the name of emergency.

Where is that loan vanished? What advantage have we accrued through those loans? What development projects have we culminated to have given respite to the people and returned some portion of that money towards reduction of that loan? Our governments and politicians instead filled their already filled corrupted pockets with that sacred money. For God sake someone has to account for spending the loans in a judicious manner and reducing the liability that we are carrying for so many years. Instead we are sinking further with this burden with no efforts to redeem. We were hoping that the new government would look after the national trust but they immediately indulged in further corruption, unnecessary foreign visits and un manageable ministerial and other appointments to further deteriorate the economy.

The present flood calamity is much bigger than the earthquake but handling much poorer than before. No one could correctly speculate the scale of disaster till it started flowing over the heads and roofs of the people. On one side the people were dyeing and most of the infrastructure being ruined, but on the other side the president was roaming around in Europe on unofficial visits, humouring his children and enjoying his property possessions. His cronies instead of advising him to return were justifying and encouraging him to continue his rampage.

The world leaders also took it as seriously as did our president till Mr. Ban Ki-Moon, the UN Secretary General took his own initiative to examine the calamity personally. He shook the world with the punch of utmost warning about the quantum of destruction. It was only then that our friends and sympathizers rose to the occasion. We should be thankful to the Americans, Saudis, Turks, and British, to extend their help more than our expectations. Other small countries were equally good to reach us with all kind of assistance. However, unfortunately because of the credibility of our leaders, they were not as generous as they were in 2005.

Monitory and other material aid is welcomed, as this is part of the world community system for assistance to all disaster-hit countries. Loan from IMF and its circle should not be accepted at any cost. We are already in deep waters up to our throat and are under debt of over fifty three billion dollars, which is likely to increase to seventy three billion in 2015. In addition we have about Rs. Three trillion internal loan. What kind of credit are we leaving for our coming generation? We must not sacrifice them for our own pleasure and leisure. Loan is a curse and everyone cannot shrug it off like **Brazil**. We appreciate condoning the existing loan or suspension of the interest for ten to fifteen years as a big favour.

We must learn to stand on our own feet and cut the cloth to our size. The government must reduce its own administrative spending to minimum. No unnecessary foreign trips of government officials. Tap your own resources to develop and live within the available means. This might bring some temporary sufferings but they must be tolerated and faced bravely. Our leaders must beget their self-respect, which is for long missing. They must get rid of their begging habits and filling their pockets. Senator **Ishaq Darr** has proposed a solid plan to meet the current situation from our own resources. There is a deep philosophy in it, which would be helpful in future to restore our dignity.

We can even tap our bank sources. I personally know there are millions of people with fixed deposits and are living on their profits. Donation of a few months profit for the flood victims will not hamper in their living style and standards. That money could be directly debited from their banks to the appropriate fund collecting agencies, of course done with their consent. Where are those who are sitting under the shade of NRO, the big national loan exempts and the land mafia and corruption experts still demanding loans from world financial agencies. This country is full of natural resources. We are self sufficient in agriculture, plenty of water, and the air is of course free gift from nature. We are rich with oil potential, about two hundred million tons of coal yet to be explored and made use of and Gwadar Sea port controlling trade routes of East Asian states and China to the rest of the world. We are indeed the gateway of South East Asia. We need some dynamic leadership to bring revolution to exploit the hidden resources of the country.

The floods have broken the back of the people of Pakistan but have not done any damage to their will power. They are ready to live in temporary hardships but save the country from long term impairment. Loan and interest on it is a slow poison and terminal disease, which they like to rescue from. Our corrupt leaders want the cash to play with the trust of the people. If you look at the loan graph of foreign agencies rising so steep, it looks as if someone is coming after our throat.

I pray our leaders wakeup and save the nation from self-execution through these loans. We will die if we have to die to save our coming generation. Don't lead us to a death trap and suicide. Life is bliss and we must live it up with dignity. We welcome the aid and assistance from our friends in this difficult time, but we don't want any loan please.

Middle East Peace Talks

3rd September 2010

It was pleasing to learn that President Obama eventually returning to one of his pledges made during election campaign. It is a welcome, better late than never step in his second year term. We indeed appreciate his efforts in spite of his environmental compulsions and opposition from the Jews lobby in the White House as the first Black President of the United States. We hope and pray that his present efforts bring some fruit to solve this problem, emanating most of the terrorism in the world. The fore most criteria must be a real justice for both Palestinians and Israelis, and no indirect favours or compassion in the light of the present ground situation. He should start where President Clinton left, which was the only reliable basis somewhere close to the justice.

No agenda as initiated by the conveners invites an unrestricted discussion embracing the entire spectrum of subject matter without any specifics. It may accomplish an overall goodwill of each party but generally the discussions go round and round without heading toward the centre point. However, it does promote some goodwill amongst the interested parties but ultimately the problem has to be directed towards every controversy one by one. Everybody understands that such complicated and deep-rooted disputes take a long time to solve but step forward is preferable than a step backward.

The sensitive disputes like this are mind searching between the affected parties and the mediators. The sideline speculations wait for the end of the talks or the communiqué. However, hints generated by the outsiders before or during such meetings are sometimes innovating and tend to change the course of events to a purposeful direction.

Justice is the first white flag that radiates confidence to the parties concerned. America may have to demonstrate this to the Israeli's and Palestinians to believe about their efforts for a peaceful solution. Traditional meetings mean nothing to them and the world. Obama may consider announcing the same pledge for Palestinians as American presidents have been openly declaring the guarantee of Israeli security;

otherwise justice may receive the same prejudice colour as the declared intensions in favour of Israel.

Two State Theory is basically a hoax. There is no other two independent adjacent States having the same type of common borders with so much of power disparity and so many conditions and restrictions laid on one to live in an un-State like State. Palestinian acceptance of such an agreement would mean to live under duress and occupation for all times to come. Gaza strip and main land West Bank seem intentionally tailored to divide Palestine into segments bound to fail as a State and remain a satellite of Israel. Those sitting as judges must uphold justice and truth after reviewing all aspects of a viable State.

Palestine as a country was shaped by nature as a one cohesive indivisible unit. The West after World War-II framed it in their own vision as an unnatural entity. They shoved the Jews to Palestine in large numbers to clear their own inventory. The Jews understandably became bigger power than the local inhabitants and occupied most of the territory with the help of their masters. This illusion might stick around for years or may be centuries but has to filter one day. Sooner it is better it is for all the parties concerned. In reality the Jews have come to stay because they have no other place to go. They have to create feeling of comradeship with the Arabs, who I think are more than willing to accommodate them. Why cant democracy prevail as a coexistent and adjustment between the two communities. With a very balanced population they can regenerate their efforts to live together peacefully. If South African Whites can find a place amongst the majority of Blacks, I am sure the Jews and Arabs with favourable equations would make a better deal of it. The Americans may stop chasing an unperceivable illusion of Two State Theory but let both the parties realistically frame an entity for themselves. Time is no constraint but during the process they must endeavour to come closer by creating of goodwill and sympathy for each other. The Palestinian would certainly need the American guarantee in case of any security breach by their powerful neighbour.

Mr. Netanyahu, maybe representing Israel but Mr. Mahmoud Abbas is indeed nobody to bargain on behalf of Palestinians majority. He is not the representative of Hamas who were elected to be in the office of authority. Any decision between Netanyahu and Mr. Abbas will not be binding on the actual incumbents, Hamas and other Palestinians. The refugees who have been rolling around the world and are keen to return to their homeland are also the big stakeholders who may not be having allegiance with Mr. Abbas. The other Arabs especially the Syrians and Lebanese who have yet to sort out their territorial disputes of 1967 war are also part of this deal that is being settled by the three parties in isolation. Al Qaeda who have been fighting the Palestinian war for all these years are sitting on the hedge watching the development. Anything going against the basic Palestinians cause may become controversial between them and need to be rectified by the Palestinians themselves.

With the present awakening in the Muslim world, especially after incident of the Turkish Flotilla in June'2010, where besides Muslims, many members of the World Human Rights organisation were killed, also looking at the outcome of these talks. Anything unacceptable to the larger faction of Palestinians would not be acceptable to them. Iranians, Iraqis, Lebanese, and Syrians are now active parties to this dispute. It is more in the interest of Israelis to settle the dispute than the Palestinians who are the real owner of the land.

This dispute, because of the American hegemony in favour of Israel has drawn almost half the world in it. It has taken the shape of a volcano, which can erupt any moment to create catastrophe. Americans would have to persuade Israelis' to reconcile with the eventual fate accompli in the interest of world peace, lest a new world order is formed which might upset the present command structure. No easy solution is possible unless a bold and commanding decision is taken by the superpower to solve this.

Barack Hussein Obama is a leader gifted by nature to lead the world. He was capable of piercing through many difficult situations like this before. He successfully handled the supremacy of White majority to his favour as a Black man in the last elections. He may go a step forward than ex president Clinton to solve the Palestinian problem, which will be a real inspiration to the world and a big favour to the Palestinian and especially to Israelis. It will certainly help get America out of Afghanistan and Iraq honourably and would indeed take her to a place it really deserves in the committee of nations. The key to Middle East peace talks is to ensure a judicious and unprejudiced conduct by all the parties irrespective of their power possessions. Mr. President; 'YES YOU CAN' do it.

Harassment of a Nuclear State

30th September 2010

Pakistan is the first Muslim nuclear state born on 14th Aug 1947 as a result of Indian partition exercised by British Raj, as planned by the Governor General of India, Lord Mount Batten, in agreement with the Red Cliff mission. The partition was basically planned on the basis of Muslim and Hindu majority populated areas. However, a few critical adjustments were manoeuvred to facilitate India with a favour to have direct access from District Gurdaspur, a Muslim majority district in East Punjab to Kashmir through courtesy of two faithful friends, Mr. Nehru and Madam Mount Batten. This was the first seed of dissentions planted by the judges of partition against a poor newly born country. The second was the influx of millions of Muslim refugees thrust from India to Pakistan.

Pakistan struggled very hard for the first ten years but thanks to field Marshal Ayub Khan's leadership that it became economically and militarily the strongest country in the region, particularly after 1965 war with India. It was only then our Western friends and Russians started a nefarious vigilance on the growing importance of Pakistan. America and the West because of Pakistan's expanding influence on the Middle East Muslim nations, engineered sanctions against all military equipment including spares and economic restrictions with the excuse of using American equipment against India. Pakistan became thirsty of even the defensive spare support and economic assistance, and Russia because Pakistan acted as a strong shield against communism, which later resulted, crucial for them in Afghanistan in 1979. Indian leadership proved most absurd for not willing to resolve Kashmir issue and they are paying for it even today. This region could have been the most affluent in the world if India had come to terms on the controversial issues on the principle of partition.

Everyone was gunning to destroy a progressive Pakistan, which could have been an asset to the development of Asia and South East Asian region. They proceeded to dismember Pakistan in 1971 through Indian, Soviet Union including our very trusted friends of military alliances.

Pakistan was broken with humiliating conditions and the desire that it could never stand in the way of all these godfathers again.

Indian jaguar hired by our faithful friends to take care of left over Pakistan in total subservient terms. God almighty had his own way of dealing with such imposters. He resurrected Pakistan stronger than before, as this was the country established to uphold his name. Chinese offered to fulfil the gap created by our friends. Pakistan recovered and got back on track of progress and development. Once again when the Soviet Union invaded Afghanistan, Americans returned to Pakistan with new love and hope to revenge their old rival. Pakistan and the Muslims from all over the world fulfilled their desire by defeating Soviets and breaking their union and alliances throughout the world. Soon after the retreat of Soviets the Americans introduced a new weapon of Pressler amendments' to harass and damage Pakistan. India became nuclear power in 1974 after conducting an initial nuclear test Operation by the name of Smiling Buddha. On May 11, 1998, *India* carried out *nuclear* tests in Pokhran. Indian leaders openly started threatening Pakistan of her existence and laying her hands off Kashmir. Pakistan had no choice but to face the death trap by the similar defense for her survival. Pakistan under compulsion became nuclear on May 20th 1998. However, she faced the wrath of the entire world except China and the Muslim states but survived the sanctions levied by the developed world.

A new wave of intimidation started from our old friends, to either eliminate Pakistan or take away the nuclear capability from her. All sorts of failed states propaganda were launched to discredit Pakistan and warn the world to deal with her at her own risk. These were the reward of services by our friends in lieu of all sacrifices rendered during Russian invasion and Afghanistan crisis.

9/11 theatre was basically an episode relating to Palestine Israel conflict. All involved were the Arabs. The alleged planners were based in America, Belgium, and Germany, at least so were the results of the cases established against some of the people. Some people firmly believe that it was planned and executed by American Jews in aid of Israel. Whosoever did it, I, in the name of humanity appeal to them not to repeat such a heinous crime because the maximum damage of it is ultimately transferred to Pakistan. Osama Bin Laden, the so-called suspect was traced out in Afghanistan as the boss man of Al Qaeda, a key figure fighting as an ally of US against the Soviets.

Taliban government refused to handover Osama as their traditional morals and offered his trial by an international court in Afghanistan. However, Mr. Bush had some other plans of crusade, which is still around the neck of America and most of her Western allies. Pakistan was forced into this war with the options of "either you are with us or against us". Instead of using Pakistan to dissuade the war, US forced her to become party to it. Whether it was intentional to involve Pakistan with a view to reach her nuclear assets was by design, but the terrorist created threats point towards destabilizing Pakistan. At the same time supporting India on Kashmir in the name of cross border terrorism against Pakistan, involving India in Afghanistan's rebuilding and trading facilities, providing India with civil nuclear assistance was a big harassment to our people especially when the same was denied to Pakistan with flimsy reason.

Pakistan is a target of terrorism for the last nine years. This has been primarily because of our involvement in the Afghan war as American ally. The tribal belt has resented our joining the war as American partner. They regard our surrender to Bush as a fake discharge and an act of unnecessary cowardice by Gen. Musharaf. That is why the tribal's have since been fighting with Pakistan army, thereby destabilizing the entire North/North Western area of Pakistan.

The country has been so disturbed because of terrorism brought through our forced involvement in American/Afghan war that no international team is ready to play cricket in Pakistan. On top of it daily drone attacks are increasing and generating hatred in the area against our armed forces and causing harassment in running day-to-day government. The result is causing chaos in Pakistan and the world is also crying about the nuclear security and mismanagement.

Putting a nuclear state against the wall is a dangerous trend. America, India, and the world must realize and refrain from such a dirty conspiracy otherwise the world might end up facing a very serious consequences bigger than 9/11, Afghanistan, and Iraq. The moment of truth has come for our good friends to realize excesses committed against Pakistan. India to understand how much both of us have lost by not coming to terms on Kashmir and other problems between us. There is a need for everyone to stop harassing Pakistan with flimsy excuses and leaving no choice for the people of Pakistan but to react and turn the entire country into a tribal society.

Mystery Surrounding Afghan War

16th October 2010

A million dollar question that haunts many of us living in this region; why were Americans arrogant to attack Afghanistan just about a month after 9/11 episode? Everybody views it in his or her own perspective. The real secret is of course known to Mr. Bush which might be disclosed one day in his memoirs. However people speculate and I stand in line to share with the world my personal views. One of the most unconvincing pursuits was in search of Osama Bin Ladin, the boss man of Al-Qaeda who could plan the operation while sitting in the caves of wild mountains with the most reliable and modern communication with highly secure secraphones un-decodable even by the most advance country of the world. The master-minds of 9/11 might one day volunteer a confession and reveal the truth about hitting the twin towers by the understudy pilots. Some consider it a joke but since it is only the one super power's quest, we might as well reluctantly compromise with their description.

Osama was readily available with the Taliban government who were willing to hand him over to an international tribunal to be tried and dealt in accordance with the decision of the court. However Mr. Bush wanted a war bounty delivered to America as a future tribute to him. It is now almost ten years that NATO forces after putting the entire Afghan soil upside down with almost 60 thousands modern A/C war sorties without finding trace of Osama. Majority of people in Pakistan believe that he is dead with no affidavit of his grave. American leadership is still hoping against hopes to find him and present him to their people. God help them in their pursuit.

Removal of Taliban government was the next aim fulfilled in a few days of war because it was a fight between an ant and the elephant. Taliban were defeated and a new govt. of northern alliance was installed against the wishes of the Pakistan govt. however it was limited to Kabul and its suburb. Taliban reorganized them selves and adopted new gorilla war tactics and are still fighting a very successful war against Americans and NATO forces. Pakistan tribal areas are also involved as the belt is a common heritage between Pakistan and Afghanistan. The people belong to the same race and have been living together with inter marriages since ages. The war has also dragged the Pakistan armed forces as ally of NATO, against the tribals for the last eight years. In addition there have been unlimited America drone attacks with casualties of many innocent people, creating more hatred towards Pakistan and America. There seems no end to this war between the allies and these rugged people who have the will and stamina to continue the fight till eternity.

Trapping Iran and having firm control of newly librated central Asian states was the only legitimate reason for coming to Afghanistan. It was probably a good way of keeping china and Russia at bay also. The methodology should have been different than the one adopted. Development of Gawadar (Baluchistan) and Afghanistan was key to this project. Destruction of Afghanistan was the last option sensible think tanks could work, even if they wanted to desert them at the end.

Reaching nuclear assets of Pakistan was another hope for Mr. Bush and his Aids, the Jewish lobby. It was an impossible task to negotiate. Destabilizing Pakistan was a dangerous adrift and an invitation to destabilize the whole region. Firstly they have been declared safe by IAEA secondly Pakistan nuclear assets are so well concealed and dispersed that even Pakistani may not be in a position to locate it easily what to talk of foreigners. It would be an exercise in futility to disturb the arrangement because it might cause another catastrophe in the world of today. A friendly Pakistan and her tribe's men are an asset to America in this region. A change of strategy in the area would be disastrous.

The remote chance of securing monopoly in drug trade could be one of Mr. Bush's hallucination like weapons of mass destruction in Iraq which took Mr. Colon Powel to convince UNO for the attack and later embarrassment for the lie. The other reason could be expectations of mineral resources out of the virgin land of Afghanistan. Only the people of America can seek and find the truth. There has been so much of blood shed in two wars that Hitler must be feeling relaxed of his crime of holocaust in addition the money wasted was good enough to inhabitate a new planet.

The funniest of all the approaches was establishing democracy in Afghanistan. A tribal society has own system of governance; little bit of democratic principles, some authoritative functions, a few anarchist tendency, and rest of it religious values and mutual respect of elders in society. Rich and poor live with equality and justice. Although the system has been polluted by mixing with modern society yet old values take precedence over so called mew civilization. King Aman Ullah tried to modernize Afghanistan and lost his kingdom. The soviets wanted to export communism and were defeated with losing their century old union and alliances of east European states. Let people live their own way of life without learning modern dirty tricks, as long as they don't interfere in other's affairs. Change; they must bring from within and in their own time frame. Red Indians and Amish are still following their own traditions inside the most modern society of USA.

The Americans were not the first and may not be the last invaders in Afghanistan. Alexander the great, Persians, Muslims, Mughals, and British failed in bringing the change. America out of them was the most civilized country with the capacity to bring a surprise but without indulging in war and destruction. However after committing this folly they had plenty of time to re-think a better change. I am sure war was not the only option nature had prescribed. Wining of heart and mind, partners in trade and developments, friends in thick and thin were better choices to share pleasure and pain together.

Pakistan is the only country outside NATO involved in this conflict. It therefore reserves the right to complain about all the damages done to her because of this war. The terrorist activities are outcome of her participation as an ally and as a result of drone attacks. The economic crises are only because of the war. The road system effected by heavy American supplies are beyond Pakistan's capacity to repair. Pakistan govt. should have asked for construction of additional motor ways for this heavy traffic from Karachi to Afghanistan before allowing of this traffic.

India on one and Iran on the other side of Afghanistan have their own axes to grind. India to ensure maximum damage to Pakistan and Iran to United States. None of them would be in favour of ending the war.

However, any attempt by friends for using India against Pakistan may reverse the whole Afghan scenario where Pakistan forces go back to east and tribals set free on west to use their own discretion. A fair distinction between friends and foes is an essential ingredient to strength. The theory of "there are no permanent friends and enemies but permanent interest only" is certainly a betrayal of friends at critical moments. Mr. Obama therefore may draw his own conclusion.

The recent peace council of elders set by Mr. Karzai and America reminds me of a Jew who was excited to win the lottery through divine concept that God once in 24hrs accepts the prayers of his people. He sat down to recitation and there came the moment of acceptance with an echo, "Mr. David at least go and buy a ticket". Peace council is welcomed to negotiate but at least be gracious to offer a unilateral ceasefire as a simple goodwill gesture to begin with.

The various factors surrounding the mystery are neither easily verifiable nor so important because the damage is already done. It is more or less an open secret. The recovery from it is vital and let us all try to get out of it. Pakistan is a bridge and a reliable link between Afghanistan and the world. A stable and strong Pakistan is a key to establish Peace in the region and guarantee to a safe passage for American exit.

The Exit of a Legend

8th May 2011

Osama Bin Laden is dead. It has been revealed by the Americans after a secret operation inside Pakistan through commando action. Some survivors from his family who could have disclosed the truth about the whole episode were taken away by the raiding party. As for today it was one-sided story how Osama and others were killed in action and their bodies taken away. Osama's death confirmation was presumably done after the DNA test and the body thrown in the sea to finish off his trace of identity from his people for good. However, his name will remain and it cannot be taken away by anyone and by any means.

Osama was a hero for whose cause he was fighting and will remain so as long as that cause exists. He stood for the Palestinians against Israel and those who supported Israel for occupation of their land. He was a nationalist of the highest order who wanted to save the wealth of his country and spend it amongst his poor countrymen. He was also a devout Muslim who was ready to fight for all Muslims fighting for the integrity and freedom of their countries. He organized and financed a big force against the Soviet Union when they invaded Afghanistan. He was one of the main elements to defeat Soviets. His dedication and sincerity affected the general Afghans so much that they refused to hand him over to Americans when accused of the liability of 9/11 attack on the twin-towers. His passion and devotion was so believed by the Afghans that they undertook the risk of facing a superpower for the sake of one man and are still fighting for the last ten years for that cause.

Apparently to the common people in Pakistan this was a big embarrassment and more so for the Pak Army from whom the people of Pakistan were feeling letdown because of a foreign force attacking inside the country and take away their bounty without our forces being aware of this operation. The point stands from the fact that the America and Pakistan forces were jointly operating against the so-called terrorist and it was therefore incumbent upon the Americans to share this operation with the Pakistan government or intelligence. Osama might have been a **vital** target but let it be known to the American bigwigs that no individual could be as vital as the relations between the two friendly countries, specially fighting a war together. With Osama gone, Al Qaeda has not vanished. It is as potent as it was with Osama and maybe more because of the loss of their leader.

Let it be known to everyone that no country in the world is capable of defending each and every house in the country from an attack of this kind. If it was so possible there would have been no 9/11 and subsequently no war in Afghanistan. As a result of such attacks, retaliation is the only consequence, which was adopted by the Americans. Our friends have trespassed in our territory without proper permission or coordination. Whether they believe it or not there is bound to be a visible or invisible retaliation from the Pak Armed Forces especially from Army and the Airforce, which might be damaging in future for the joint operations in this area. I would personally advise our friends to take care of it and apologize as soon as possible for a blunder they have committed.

In this context I would like to educate my countrymen that the peace time Air Defence deployment are different than the emergency deployment. I am not aware of the situation in this area. I thought this did not fall under enemy threat because of the joint operation with friends. I am not sure whether some radars are deployed and therefore jamming of radars is just a gossip more than the actuality. However, I would like to assure my countrymen that in peace or war our **vital** targets are effectively covered and defended at all times. Osama's house or even the army academy did not fall under this category. America or any other country's forces approaching a vital target will be dealt with as a real enemy. Similarly our ground forces are deployed to destroy the strongest forces before they could even eye on such targets. Pakistan has, by the grace of God one of the best Air Defence systems in the world and is capable of handling such emergencies with great perfection. However, if the friends are out to deceive you are likely to fall in the trap; but that is once only. The speculations and gestures of some of our political leaders that India could take this chance as a precedent are totally baseless and demoralizing. As a retired officer I feel, the doctrine of retaliation would be exercised in case of India, even if they target some shanty huts in Pakistan.

The American operations and its outcome has been the most disgusting and out of the book. Killing such evidence is the last option. Destroying vital evidence is losing the battle if not the war. Alive Osama and his associates was the key to deal with Al Qaeda, if that was the aim. Dead Osama means any eminent person dead in the battle. Al Qaeda at present was probably a spent force. However, there were many stems growing out of its roots, like Taliban who were the main force in Afghanistan and hard line Muslims in Sudan, Egypt, Iran, Yemen, and Syria.

United States had discovered Osama from Saudi Arabia, and sent him to assist Afghans against the invasion of Soviets in 1979. That is where Osama established his credential as a freedom fighter and also became the darling of the Afghans and the Muslim world. This was the time when United States could have taken a lead to negotiate with Osama to reduce tension in the Middle East and eliminate terrorism to a great extent. Instead they elected to abandon the war scene altogether and let the state of affairs take their own course.

Pakistan is being accused of playing a double game by the US. It couldn't be more ridiculous and repulsive than this. These insensible people may understand that Pakistan is a big country with one hundred and eighteen million people. It is difficult to keep track of every individual. Those who are hiding are as clever and capable as the intelligence agencies, looking for them. It takes time to search out a small insect from the sea. After all who captured Sheikh Mohammed, Libi and seven hundred others handed over to Americans. Imagine if all these were not handed over what would be the condition of the so-called war of terror. There is nothing perfect in this world. It may take one day, one year, or ten years depending on the chance to strike. The lead to find this house was also given by ISI.

Osama Bin Laden denied of taking any part in 9/11. I personally believe that, because he was not the material to deny if he had done so. You cannot always weigh everyone according to your own scale. Unfortunately the American think-tanks tow the popular lines or command guidance and mislead their nation to get into the trouble they often pick up because of their own follies.

Osama was considered a symbol of freedom in the Muslim world. Born in a rich family and brought up like a prince in Saudi Arabia. He was educated and instead of enjoying a princely life like other rich debouches, decided to dedicate his life for the suppressed Muslims. His first target was Israel, who was forcing a reign of terror on the Palestinians. He also decided to fight against those who were supporting Israel in this horrendous alliance. Some of his terrorist like activities in Kenya, Lebanon, and Saudi Arabia were part of this strategy against the alliance with Israel. Osama was used by the United States in the Afghan Soviet war. He was mindful of that but the situation coincided with his own objective. He was not the man to be used and thrown away. He always kept his main aim insight and after the war returned to his real aim and aspiration. I wish the Americans availed that opportunity to utilize his services to a good cause. They unfortunately were the slaves of their power and the power took them where they belong.

I wish Pakistan had not picked up the sin of this gruesome murder at its soil. It will always haunt our younger generation for this crime, and the soul of Osama, the martyr looking down at us with big desolate eyes, in surprise.

Major players behind the Afghan War

12th June 2011

Afghan—American war is running in eleventh year now and is so far the longest war in the US history. I am sure many big historians must be busy searching for the real causes of this war, irrespective of the specifics provided by the rulers to commence this heinous venture, to be put on record for the future generations to know the truth. The details that followed this conflict where millions of innocent human lives were lost, who had nothing to do with any of the evil deeds planned by none other than their own leaders. They were simply a collateral damage of the whims of some of these devils playing with the lives of those who had elected to accept their command voluntarily.

9/11 was a bombshell being planned for a long time and was implemented when the emotions were high and men of authority could be easily misled and misdirected towards the clash of faith and societies. The evil planners only needed a person like Mr. Bush who probably already possessed these germs to initiate turmoil in the world to register his name like his old friend Hitler. He framed charges to attack Afghanistan and forced Gen. Musharaf of Pakistan to join so that later on Pakistan was included to this process of destruction. Iraq was falsely dragged into such an operation through the fraud reports about WMD (weapons of mass destruction). This whole thing was probably part of the plan conceived by a few to accrue benefit out of this power play.

Soviet Union was defeated in Afghanistan in 1989 by Allah, the almighty, through insignificant crowd of Osama Bin Laden, Afghan Mujahideen selected out of the refugees and of course pick of Pakistan Army to train organize and plan all operations. In the beginning the Indians and others thought it was a joke to face this mighty force with a small group of riffraff. But when results started taking control of the situation in favour of resistance, everyone was astonished to experience this miracle. India was the only country in the free world supporting the Soviets, not for their love or success but to see Pakistan humiliated and crushed, and they kept attached to their expectations till the end. They thought Pakistan was in front of the tornado and would soon be trampled but 'man proposes and God disposes'. The situation soon developed to see Pakistan in the driving seat and Soviets going back shattered and disintegrated. Mr. Bush of course knew this reality like a Gospel truth, but always kept India in the list of beneficiary in spite of their conspiratorial attributes. When Soviets were defeated India became more apprehensive about Pakistan's ability and capacity. They started planning the new strategy to continue their gambit against Pakistan in cahoots with America.

American leadership sometimes behaves like an absolute naïve while implying things towards their bias without proper investigation and political scrutiny. I don't think they review the history while dealing with other people/nations. People go through the pedigree even while playing dog and horse races. The British strictly believed in this, and in India always went through the pedigree even selecting the soldiers in their army. The Americans may be shy of their past when most of the undesirables were forced to immigrate out of Europe to America. Mr. Bush presumably played in the hands of India to attack Afghanistan without carrying out a proper research. He totally ignored Pakistan's suggestion to negotiate with Taliban government for a suitable outcome, but instead forced Gen. Musharaf to join in the war with a bogey of Indian false intensions of teaming up. The foolish General gave in and made Pakistan to suffer for the last ten years without acknowledgment and realization from America for our complete economic collapse and tremendous loss of life. India is still pursuing the same strategy and has established at least six consulates between Mazar-e-Sharif and Kandahar with the connivance of America to destabilize Pakistan in Baluchistan and tribal areas. It is specifically done so that Pakistan is kept away from claiming Kashmir and China is deprived of any support in this region. The Americans must know that the people of Pakistan are aware of such malicious designs. On top of this America pressurized Pakistan to accept ground trade links with Afghanistan through India. How can people of Pakistan reconcile from within when they see a partisan behaviour and action from a friend towards our enemy.

Unfortunately America is playing the Indian game because of the China bogey or otherwise. However, I think America knows that India is one of the major players indirectly responsible for stretching this war in Afghanistan to damage Pakistan. Let it be known to both that it is neither in the hands of India nor America to accomplish this task. The one who created this country has the responsibility to protect and keep it going. It is not a myth but a belief like American reality of 1492.

There is no doubt in anyone's mind including America that Indians are financing the Baloch youth to revolt against the government and every now and then there are acts of sabotage, bombing government assets, killing and looting in the province. After all from where this huge quantity of arms and ammunition, ration, and other support equipment coming from, it is either Indian or American provisions. Someone has to catch the truth and put an end to this bluff of hypocrisy.

Al Qaeda is another bluff causing serious tensions and future visionary security hazards to America. Its basic aim was to fight for the cause of Palestinians against Israel but it has been so cunningly misconstrued by Israel and American Jews towards reflecting perpetual danger to America and her people. The American leadership has been so dubiously led to accept it as a truth for their survival. The Jews have so cleverly ingrained this concept that there seems no place left in American brain cells to notice the deadly germs implanted by this alien agency to disrupt their peaceful life and in turn the lives of the other half of the world. The Americans have unfortunately made it mandatory on themselves to support Israel against poor Palestinians. If they had so much of love for the Jews they should not have allowed Europeans to export them to grab a foreign land in the Middle East. However there were some saner elements like PM (late) Yitzhak Rabin who wanted to make up but was assassinated by the Jews themselves to ditch the Oslo accord and Mr. Clinton's plan of establishing peace failed thereafter. Mr. Bush then took over and made monkey deal out of the justice, like he manoeuvred his own election results with Mr. Al Gore. It is time for Americans for a fresh evaluation of the Palestinian problem with a just mind to conclude. Otherwise the influential Jews who kept leading them towards their own Juke-box and steered them towards 9/11, Iraq, Iran, Afghanistan, and Pakistan. The point to note is that the tree of terrorism was initially planted at Palestine by Europe and later promoted by America in the whole of Middle East. This very tree has become a jungle and exported to half of the world. It needs to be re-examined and checked otherwise it will eat up the grower and the users. The road to peace starts from Jerusalem and passes through Tel Aviv to Gaza and everyone should be entitled to use it without paying any toll tax. There is no other legitimate route. The Jews have the choice to accept it now or after hundred years. The best for them is to learn from South Africa and enjoy the world now. There is no wisdom in going back to Europe after hundred years.

The American leadership must realize the destruction they have caused their own innocent people and their so-called enemies from a false alarm and baseless excuse of 9/11. No one can finish America as long as her three hundred million people are awake, her fifty states are intact and their charity for the poor world persists. My holy Prophet, Mohammad (PBUH) regarded charity a bliss that saves you from many evils. Barak Hussein Obama knows this and is dying to work for the poor but as a black president he is aware of his limitations and intentions of the White elite and Jews lobby whose tiny minority has made the poor American majority a hostage of their so-called economy and survival, A gimmick.

India and Israel have a common cause and their collusion is understandable. They are therefore successfully promoting to keep this war going. It is up to Americans to realize and resolve the mess they have created in Iraq, Afghanistan, and Pakistan. The Middle East story has though gone in the background in face of the current crises but still has a pivotal role in eliminating terrorism in the world.

THE JEERING PRESIDENT AND THE OPPOSITION

26th June 2011

A recent exchange of fire between the two big leaders created a real commotion in the country. Mr. Nawaz Sharif was running an election campaign in Azad Kashmir and obviously needed a fire work on the sitting government to win support of the people affected by the wrong policies of the government. The weakness of the ruling party was his main target and I think he was very frank in transmitting it to the people without getting personal at any of the top officials. Bad governance, corruption, mismanagement, poor or no foreign policies, internal and external insecurities of the country and above all death and terrorism emanating out of the above follies of the government. I personally think it was his right to talk to the people and convince them about the need to change.

Mr.Zardari, the president was not very comfortable about the accusation made by Mr. Nawaz Sharif and he had to dig out something drastic to reciprocate and neutralize the malice disseminated to the people. As a politician this was his right to clear his position but unfortunately he was the president of Pakistan and he had to be cognizant of his neutral image and obligation towards the opposition. He not only failed to realize but also became vulgar and impertinent, showing complete disrespect to the status and stature of the president of Pakistan.

This whole debate reminded me of my college days where annual debates between the college competitive clubs used to demonstrate their student like display of behavior during the contest. In 1950s Gordon College Rawalpindi was known for literary contest in whole of Pakistan. Its Minerva and Bar clubs were famous for the debates. At least once a year we had debate contestants from all over Pakistan and those few nights were the most interesting festival in the college. During speeches we witnessed all kinds of catcalls, howling and jeering from the opponents from their sides of the seating. Who won and lost was not the criteria but who put up the best show and arguments was the memories at least for one year till, the commencement of the next year.

What we saw at Naodero during the august speech of Mr. Zardari on the occasion of Benazir's birthday anniversary presented nothing less than the college hall when we saw mimicking of the person no less than the president of Pakistan. I can never forget in my life such a parody till a better one comes up, next year. Jeering of the president was truly like a caricature matching and complimenting the student's actions during debates.

Benazir was a very intelligent political figure and knew the character and political vision of her husband. That was the reason she had opted him out of country politics otherwise she would have brought him back, with her after her long exile out of Pakistan. She also did not include him in any of the negotiations with opposition specifically during signing of COD (charter of democracy) and NRO negotiation with Gen. Musharaf. Whether she was discussing with him at home is a question needs to be clarified from her very close friends like Nahid Abbasi and good PPP affiliates of that time. Whether Mr. Zardari was in line of inheritance in Benazir's books is not known, neither is authenticated by any of her very close associates. That is why her will has no real credence for Mr.Zardari. The present cronies of PPP around Mr. Zardari are of no significance in this context.

Mr. Nawaz Sharif was at times crossing limits of decencies in the heat of the moments during political gatherings specially talking against the Arm forces. His personal experience with Gen. Musharaf was not to be applied universally with all other generals. He has to be discreet in addressing the army, our national asset. Zardari was right in pointing out Mr. Sharifs disrespect to the Army. He has talked about it many times before and his party has made it a habit to ridicule the army in public. I hope he realized, that enough was enough.

Nodero was a gathering to remember Benazir and her achievements for the nation. It was a day to pray for her and highlight her services to the people of Pakistan. It was not an excuse to jeer at the opponents who could be pushed in retaliation causing aspersions on her weakness and exploits for her family. After all Mr. Zardari and his children are relishing today because of her some of the things that she or he capitalized during her rule.

Mr. Zardari is now president of Pakistan, his expression of Nawaz Sharifs cast as a 'lohar' was the most unbecoming of the stature of the president. All citizens are equal constitutionally no matter what cast they belong to. Those who work and earn for Pakistan are much better than those who live on commission and defraud and are known to be Mr. ten percent and product of NRO. Politics is not about the cast but the personality, character, honour, respect and leadership qualities.

I have personally no affiliation with Nawaz League but Mr. President's speech was most objectionable, especially when he was jeering and making faces in sarcasm while talking about Mr. Nawaz Sharif. As president this was indeed very disgusting particularly while mentioning about the 'character of democracy', mastermind of the one in whose honour anniversary was being commemorated at Naodero. I cannot help quoting verses of a poet:

JAHIL KO AGAR JEHL KA INAAM DIA JAEY

ISS HAADESA-E-WAQAT KO KIA NAAM DIA JAEY

MAIY KHAANAY KI TOHIN HAY RINDOON KI HATAK HAY

KAM-ZARF KE HATHUN MEI AGAR JAAM DIA JAEY

(If a fool is rewarded for his daftness what name is suited to this kind of misfortune? It is insult to a pub or pub affiliates if a glass of wine is entrusted to a niggardly fellow.)

Heading Towards a Dangerous Showdown

26ᵗʰ May2011

Abbottabad was a melting point that created a highest degree of mistrust between two friends fighting a war of terror for the last ten years. It was indeed the biggest crack or breach caused that seemed certainly heading towards a dangerous showdown. War of words was an immediate sequel that followed from both sides, Americans talking of stopping of the aid and Pakistan pulling out of the coalition. This relationship right from the beginning was contentious where the people of Pakistan did not like to pursue American motives, to kill or catch Osama Bin Laden or defeat Taliban government in Afghanistan. The union was brought by force where Pakistan was a hostage to join the coalition and were threatened with dire consequences for not doing so. This indeed signifies the foundation of comradeship laid by Mr. Bush, the then president of USA.

This enforced relationship drove Pakistan as an ally to this war. Slowly and slowly this American war involuntarily turned out into our own war and we became the victim of this dictated arrangement. Pakistan thus became a partner, fighting against the Taliban (our old friends) and foreign elements retreating from Afghanistan to tribal areas of Pakistan. We also undertook to help maintain permanent supply lines for the NATO forces occupying Afghanistan, to eliminate Al-Qaeda and their allies engaged in fighting against the NATO occupation forces.

Soon the new facet of war shifted its nucleus from Afghanistan to Pakistan with an excuse of insurrection in tribal areas. A series of drone attacks started unilaterally by US forces inside Pakistan, which killed more innocent civilians than the so-called insurgents. An American requested organized attack of Pakistan army in South Waziristan brought a new wave of hostilities against Pakistan and there started a series of suicide bombers in every corner and small cities of Pakistan, as retaliation to these drone attacks in Northern and South Waziristan.

Americans are now sitting on the hedge in Afghanistan, watching the actual war scenario in Pakistan. However, there is one odd attack here and there by the Taliban contingents in Afghanistan. The expenses of only keeping vigilance in Afghanistan is around 1 billion dollars a month, where Pakistan government share for actually fighting the war is nearly 1.2 billion yearly. Pakistan bears the additional burden from its own resources. Because of this there is a new wave of economic and national insecurity visible at every walk of life causing grave instability in Pakistan.

Osama Bin Laden has been found and killed, a new so-called democratic government installed in Afghanistan since almost five years. The purpose of bringing war to Afghanistan has been achieved. Little bit of trouble here and there should be sorted out with the passage of time. It is time for the Americans to have fresh appraisal of the situation. Chasing Al Qaeda remnants and Taliban in Pakistan is neither their prerogative nor responsibility. Instead it is causing an unnecessary rift between two friends, resulting into a dangerous level of conflict over the sovereignty of Pakistan. There has already been a split of views over the Osama operation.

After Abbottabad incident there was a stern reaction from public, and the parliament of Pakistan had to pass some tough resolutions to be followed. The American response was not very conciliatory and two drone attacks immediately followed killing about fifteen people and injuring scores of them. It seemed an intentional violation of the parliament orders. The general behaviour of the American officials was also unfriendly, rather belligerent.

Under the circumstances, Mr. Bush's doctrine, "either you are with us or against us", seems in jeopardy. However, the war is not an option at all. For Pakistan it will be the last, rather a dying course of action. I am sure it will also be very inconvenient for America. It may be a treat to India and Israel who are pushing America to do it, but if they were wise, they would stay away from this. Pakistan has many options to deal with them separately and effectively. As for America, we have tremendous disparity. We might be shown a stone-age scenario yet it would not be very convenient for Americans. They have also one hundred and thirty thousand troops with all the supporting elements in Afghanistan. History is very cruel and sometimes repeats itself. British have a very sad experience of Afghan wars during the 19th century, and they know how many of their fighting troops returned from these hostile hills. Somewhere in 1842, twelve thousand British troops were left to fight in Afghanistan; only one, Dr. William Briden returned or was sent back as a witness. Some skirmishes continued and there was nothing but defeat for the invading forces. It was indeed the continuation of the same journey of history in 1989 which broke up the Soviet Union. This new kickoff after 9/11 was no different. The war was forced on Taliban with an excuse of catching Osama and then after the intention was to finish off the war in a few days. At least this was the message to General Musharaf at that time with the promise that the Northern Alliance would return to Mazar-e-Sharif. The war is on since then and only God knows its conclusion. However, one thing has been identical, the character and behaviour of the tribal's on both sides of Pakistan and Afghanistan. They always fought for and against each other at will but settled down as one entity at the end according to the prevailing conditions.

It is interesting to note that whenever things deteriorate beyond tolerable limits, sometimes our friend Senator John Kerry comes and settles half the score; sometimes Hillary Clinton comes and comforts things with her charm and quick-witted shrewdness. However both are tasked to make fool of our corrupt political leadership whose character ratings are on their fingertips and they sense their inside strength. The Pak army leadership has decided to stay away from power politics because they now understand that all our political angels ultimately make fool of the simple uneducated masses who stand with them to blame the armed forces at the end even when their sincerity is beyond controversy.

After Vietnam, America has not tasted any solid setback from any civil or military force. It appears that they want to break that record of constant achievements. We have been comrade against communism in SEATO and CENTO, coordinated operations against Soviets with U-2 reconnaissance aircraft, and Afghan-Russia war of 1979 with complete success. We needed our friends once in 1971 but were let down. It would be indeed desirable not to make it a habit of betraying friends at all time.

Wise is the one who can visualize the future and come out of it with honour, not the one who meets the consequence of doom. I am sure our old friends would not embark upon a suicidal mission, and we of course would hate to take advantage of their vulnerability. Friends do keep regards and semblance of grace even when they are forced through circumstances to end up in a situation like this. People are fed-up of this cat and rat race and like to get out of this position before it reaches a point of no return and becomes susceptible to a dangerous showdown.

God bless Pakistan, America, Afghanistan, and Taliban. Let us all fight terrorism together and track down the real source without prejudice. We all know its origin. Talking is the prescription whether it is Al-Qaeda, or Israel. We should stop both of them from walking on the wrong side of the road. Let Mr. Obama be the traffic sergeant and force both Al-Qaeda and Mr. Netanyahu follow the traffic rules. That would automatically reduce tension in most part of the globe.

My friend Ahmad Faraz's (late) Urdu verses are true picture of the current situation,

"BURBAAD KAR KAY BASRA 'O BAGHDAD KA JAMAAL
AB CHASHMAY BADD HAI JANBE KHYBER LAGI HUEI
GHAIRON SE KIYA GILLA HO KAY APNNO KAY HAATH SE
HAI DOSEROON KI AAG MERAY GHAR LAGI HUEI"

(After defacing the beauty of Basra and Baghdad the eyes of the devil are now gunning towards Khyber. There is no reason for us to complain because we have ourselves burnt our house with other's fire).

About the Author
Gp. Capt. (R) Rab Nawaz Choudhry

The author was born and raised in a village, Tarlai Kalan, close to modern day Islamabad, the capital of Pakistan. The author spent his childhood in an environment of love, peace, and friendship. There was very little education, but everybody was helpful and was "comrades in arm" to one another. Human rights violations were marginal as compared to the present day. Perhaps that is why there was no need to have any organization looking after this aspect of life. However, as education and lust for money increased, the violence in different forms also found its way into the normal and natural way of life. Modern education must be human-oriented rather than country, leader, and stomach-oriented. The intellectuals and educators must work to reduce or eliminate the element of selfishness, self-interest, materialism, and deception.

The author joined Pakistan Air Force Academy in March, 1953 and received his commission as a pilot in June, 1955. However, he hardly flew as a pilot and was soon sent to the United States to study an emerging field called "Air Defense." With a few colleagues, author returned to Pakistan and established an Air Defense system, an element which was completely missing in the Pakistan Air Force. This was the beginning of 1958 and by the grace of God the Almighty; Pakistani Air force was able to establish a credible Air Defense system to meet the challenges of the modern Air Defense warfare in those days. The system proved its success when the author intercepted an Indian Air Force Canbera

227

Aircraft and shot down while on a reconnaissance mission to Pakistan. This was the first kill to prove that the Pakistan Air Defense system had achieved its adolescence.

The Air Force life, experiences, and travel helped the author to meet many people from various nationalities around the world. The author learned from some, disseminated what he knew to some, and exchanged knowledge, ideas, and experiences with others; these diverse groups included people from the Armed Forces of the USA (Americans), UK (British), France, Germany, Spain, Turkey, Russia, and Iran. According to the author, the time he spent in the Middle East was some of the best experiences in his life. These include the Air Forces of Iraq, Jordan, Syria, Egypt, and UAE. In fact, he learned a great deal from the aforementioned countries and people.

After his retirement from the Air Force in 1980 the author elected to do business. He successfully developed relationship with some of the internationally renowned companies among which most of them were the renowned American companies. Politics was the last field of his choice. He fought for elections for the National Assembly of Pakistan from Islamabad in 2001.

Author was very disturbed by the 9/11 incident and felt the pain of American loss and subsequently coalition attack on Afghanistan and Iraq which resulted in loss of numerous innocent human lives. As a consequence, Author wrote the first book Terrorism or Awakening in 2005. Book had great reviews by the newspapers and foreign Ambassadors in Pakistan, which can be viewed on his website www. terrorismawakening.com

The author's diverse experience in life reveals that human relations and mutual respect is a key to success. His investment in life remains his family and friends irrespective of any preference to race, religion, and nationality. The journey will continue and so will be life.

AMBASSADOR
OF THE REPUBLIC OF INDONESIA

May 20, 2005.

Mr. Rab Nawaz Chaudhry
Rawalpindi.

Dear Mr. Nawaz!

Thank you very much for sending the very informative and well-written book *"Terrorism or Awakening"*. The book carries in-depth study of the problem of terrorism with a different perspective and the thought and content of the book is commendable.

With my renewed thanks for your kindness, please accept my best wishes.

Yours sincerely

Anwar Santoso

Indonesia Embassy
Islamabad - Pakistan

T/218   24 May 2005

Dear Mr. Chaudhary,

I would like to thank you for kindly supplying me with a copy of your book "Terrorism or Awakening."

I agree with you wholeheartedly in the belief that all countries must do their part to not only reduce the ugly reality of terrorism, but to eradicate it altogether from our world.

Your efforts in writing this book and addressing difficult questions will, I hope, prove very useful in the ongoing fight against terrorism. I appreciate your having shared your thoughts with me.

Best Regards,

Nobuaki Tanaka
Ambassador of Japan

Mr. Rab Nawaz Chadhary
142 Race Course Road,
Rawalpindi

British
High Commission
Islamabad

Diplomatic Enclave
Ramna 5
P.O. Box 1122
Islamabad

Telephone: 822131/5
Telegrams: Prodrome, Islamabad
Telex: 54122 (a/b 54122 UKEMB PK)
Facsimile: 823439

From the High Commissioner, Mark Lyall Grant CMG

14 June 2005

Group Captain (Retd) Rab Nawaz Choudhary,
142 Race Course Road,
Rawalpindi

Dear Group Captain.

Many thanks for your letter and book "Terrorism or Awakening". I have not had a chance to read it in detail yet, but I look forward to doing so. I agree that advanced countries have their part to play in reducing terrorism. The United Kingdom is committed to helping build capacity in a number of Pakistani law enforcement agencies. We are also engaged in very substantial development work in Pakistan.

Her Majesty's Government is heavily engaged in the Middle East peace process at present. We took a very active role in the campaign to protect Bosnia ten years ago.

British Muslims are represented in Parliament, the professions and the arts. We take pride in the successful inter-faith relations in the UK, and I hope these can serve as a model internationally. We will continue to play our part in encouraging reconciliation.

Many thanks for your contribution on this subject, which dominates the inernational scene at present.

Yours sincerely,

Mark Lyall Grant